INTERMEDIATE
VOLUME 2

How to Read the Akashic Records

Expanded Insights & Techniques for Accessing the Records

with

Bill Foss

The Akashic Records Center
Institute For Higher Learning

© 2019 Bill Foss All Rights Reserved

Acknowledgements:

I would like to thank everyone who has contributed to the workshops and classes their time, resources and personal support during the past years of teaching abroad and during the production and constant vigilance in writing, publishing and producing these books. Also to all the practitioners, teachers and holy masters who have changed the world for the better with their presence, service and teachings and have made a personal impact on my life and the lives of countless others with continued inspiration for creativity, service, and healing.

Note: The information and exercises contained within this book are not intended to replace psychological counselling or medical attention. If you feel the need for help, contact a qualified service professional in the appropriate field. Do not attempt to engage in the meditation, visualization, or energy exercises in this book while operating tools, heavy machinery or a motor vehicle.

ISBN-13: 978-1-7339358-0-7 (White Wizard Publishing)

ISBN-10: 1-7339358-0-0 "How to Read the Akashic Records"
Vol. 2 Intermediate
© 2019 Bill Foss World All Rights Reserved

TABLE OF CONTENTS

1. WELCOME TO THE AKASHIC RECORDS 1
2. THE TAPESTRY OF SOULS 11
3. WINDOWS TO THE COSMOS 21
4. THE MOSAIC FLOOR 31
5. THE BOOK OF LIFE 39
6. THE MYSTICAL MIRROR 49
7. MUSIC OF THE SPHERES 61
8. THE ROOMS AND SECTIONS 75
9. THE UPPER CHAMBER 83
   EXERCISE 1 TOUR OF THE AKASHIC RECORDS 93
   EXERCISE 2 SRI YANTRAM LEFT-RIGHT BRAIN 103
10. ANCESTRAL HEALING 111
    EXERCISE 3 WINDOW TO ETERNITY 119
    EXERCISE 4 ALTERNATE NOSTRIL BREATHING 127
11. STARTING TO WORK WITH CRYSTALS 133
12. EARTH PORTALS TO THE AKASHIC RECORDS 143
    EXERCISE 5 JOURNEY TO THE EARTH RECORDS 149
13. ENERGIZING, EXPANDING AND CLEARING 157
14. BELIEVING, TRUSTING & KNOWING 169
15. BENEFITS FROM ENTERING THE AKASHA 177
16. RELEASING EMOTIONAL PAIN & FEAR 187
    EXERCISE 6 INNER CHILD, LIFETIME 195
    EMOTIONAL HEALING
17. JOURNEY HOME TO THE ETERNAL MOMENT 203
    EXERCISE 7 COSMIC EXPANSION PROCESS 209
    TEACHING TERMS 219
    GLOSSARY 225
    PRODUCTS & SERVICES 262

Dedication

May this Book Serve You
In Your Search for
Greater Understanding
as You Look Into
Dreams, Visions and Intuitions.
With Eyes that can See
and Ears that can Hear,
For You, the Reader,
And to All the
Workshop Sponsors & Participants
the World Over, Thanks for Helping to Make
This Book a Reality,
I Hope It Serves You Well, Enjoy!

INTERMEDIATE
VOLUME 2

HOW TO READ THE AKASHIC RECORDS

EXPANDED INSIGHTS & TECHNIQUES FOR ACCESSING THE RECORDS

WITH BILL FOSS

THE AKASHIC RECORDS CENTER
INSTITUTE FOR HIGHER LEARNING

© 2019 Bill Foss World All Rights Reserved

Introduction

As we move deeper into the material, you will now be able to glimpse the detailed immensity of the Akashic Records. The vast regions of knowledge, wisdom and information that can be gained from a well rounded and balanced approach to accessing the higher mind.

We start this volume with a detailed description of the Akashic Hall of Wisdom. The different levels. the dynamics and energetic mechanisms that are available for our use in our continued inquiries into the Records.

From the tapestries of Souls and Lifetimes to the Mosaic Floors. The transparent field containing the walls, windows and doorways. The different sections and the upper chamber. So many unique creative archetypical approaches to trigger and inspire the different levels of the mind.

You will also realize the need for going through the Beginning stages of Volume 1 as we trek into new territory. Now it all starts to make sense at a deeper level as we continually take new levels of inventory. The common theme is growth, interactive participation, advanced mind study and learning on a Soul level about energetic activations and inter-dimensional perspective reference points.

There is no right or wrong way to learn, advance or move forward in your studies. One person will get it one way and another person will get another key at another time and juncture. That's what makes us all unique in our studies. So don't be alarmed if you are slow to start or even move ahead into uncharted territories.

As you are moving ahead the key is to relax, let go and let it unfold for you. You may go back over simple parts and procedures that can hold deep insights for you. Remember that in many of the ancient classical studies the higher truths are often hidden in the simplicities of the beginning levels of the teachings.

This is a certain teaching style that also preserves the authenticity of the messages and teachings as well as continually produces naturally new basic approaches for each student. The messages and insights can be a central template providing continually creative approaches for all students. This will be integrative to our continued work within the Akashic Records. And after a while you may develop your own style which is stand alone or that you can use along with whatever your natural energetic gift may be. So you can use the Akashic Records along with any other healing modality whether formally announced or naturally integrated behind the scenes as your own reference tool.

There will be many new perspectives which we will build upon and these will also form a foundation for the 3rd Volume. There will also be several new exercises you can use to stimulate and activate your mental acuity, soul awareness and intuitive powers.

This is a life long process that you're embarking upon. Something that you will always have as part of your higher perspectives whether you choose to continually use it or just pull it out from time to time and look through it. Which ever way that it unfolds for you it will be perfect in the moment.

You will also have the opportunity in this volume of work to engage and complete deeper levels of clearing and healing. Release and momentum can happen for you as you feel free and lighter in your body, mind and spirit to move forward in the perfect way of choosing for your life. So let's get started together and I'll see you in the Records!

Best Regards & Many Blessings of Light!
Bill Foss 12/29/2018

x

INTERMEDIATE
VOLUME 2

How to Read the Akashic Records

Expanded Insights & Techniques for Accessing the Records

with Bill Foss

The Akashic Records Center
Institute For Higher Learning

© 2019 Bill Foss All Rights Reserved

A WAY STATION FOR ALL SOULS VISITING THE EARTH THROUGH INCARNATIONS. A PLACE OF VISITATION, LEARNING AND RETREAT BETWEEN SENTIENT LIFETIMES.

Chapter 1
Welcome to the Akashic Records

When we think about the Akashic Records, it may conjure many different ideas, visions or pictures of other worldly or inter-dimensional places. Some constructs are dream like and others are very lucid. This place is very accessible though just out of sight and just out of reach. The Akashic Records is all of this and much more.

Ever streaming with new considerations of energy for creation through the group mind of humanity as well as the minds of individuals. A way station for all souls visiting the earth through incarnations. A place of visitation, learning and retreat between sentient lifetimes.

Existing from deep within the Mother Earth, across the surface terrain and up into the outer atmosphere are the connecting points and passage ways for entry. Could it be said that the Akashic Records is a part of the etheric field of Mother Earth? Yes. The Earth is a living being that is conscious of all beings here as part of nature. Though, the Akashic Records library system is also part of what we consider to be part of heaven. A dimensional place that is spatial in nature and has the ability to move, morph and change through archetypical imagery within the constructs of the higher mind. It is hidden until it is looked into at which time it becomes interactive.

Many of us have uniquely different experiences that are creatively personal in our own observation, and many of us have similar experiences of imagery which others have reported to experience. In this way the Akasha is an interactive sensory library of souls and a repository of time space events pertaining to everything of earthly planetary nature.

The matrix of all Souls interacting with the earth, each other and connecting up through the over souls and the monads back to Source and into the Akashic Records. Each Soul group comprised of 12 Souls, 12 Soul groups connected together through an Over Soul. 12 Over Soul groups all connected together with an Over Over Soul. Continuing in progression up into what is referred to as the **Monad** which is a Soul expression form of Creator God Source Light Energy. And in turn this Light Monad is connected directly back to that Light of Creator God Source.

Welcome to the Akashic Records

Each one of these groups as well as each one of the individual Souls are simultaneously linked into the Akashic Records library where each Soul has it's own repository of thoughts, word and deeds called a **Book of Life**, which we will also refer to as the Book of Lifetimes.

Simple and classic in nature if approached by an individual person for the humble sake of healing or self knowledge, though more complex the more you go into it at deeper levels and start to see, feel and experience the immensity of what's available there. In this way it is an advanced system that knows how to simplify for an inquiring mind or how to move that mind forward as they're ready for deeper study. Much like Universal energy, the Akashic Records (also comprised of the same energy) is consciously aware that it is being looked at and interacts accordingly.

There are many subtle pathways into the Akasha. We will utilize in this book the visual and textural descriptions so that you can get your mind into the concepts of it. The similarly aligned pathways, though placed uniquely in different ways through the individual mind, the group mind, the human heart, the deep earth, the sky and the outer and upper atmospheres of the planet are accessible in such a way that you may use them to create interactively, study, heal, or to remember. You may also travel past, present or future bound along the time space event horizon. These aspects and qualities are representational of the Akasha or Sky

Library. You might say that the Akashic Records is the original 'cloud'.

This is the organic road to Self knowing and the intuitive arts. Always accessible for each and every earthbound or out of body Soul visiting the planet. Also containing the streaming information of any and every moment experienced. A virtual organic living memory bank for every person, place and thing. To kindly access these great banks with reverence will serve you well. The Akasha responds well to peaceful entry and not conflict.

The joint venture that the Akasha and You have in common is your learning through experiences here on the earth plane in order to come to a sense of completion and move in new creative directions on an evolutionary pathway in new incarnations beyond this planet including new worlds and new dimensions.

So you really can only imagine what it might be like until you experience it for yourself. Many times we often try to explain the dynamics around a certain energy or spiritual exercise and the words become a shallow repetitive template or a deeply philosophical idea so much that we can only scratch the tip of the prophetic iceberg. This is why so many words are used and sometimes the same words or expressions seem to fall short, though in hopes that humanity will connect to Spirit through those messages. As we continue to elaborate in hopes that the messages will creatively reach the ears, eyes, minds and hearts of humanity.

The higher energies of the cosmos and the organically natural high vibrational beings that are coming through with messages in this material at this time want to make sure that the organic approach for all of us and our Soul's journeys are preserved and provided for in a continually streaming naturally giving and spiritual manner. So onwards and upwards let the journey continue as we begin the next approach to the Akashic Records in this 2nd volume of 3.

Welcome to the Akashic Records

So as we begin our colorful descriptive journey, this will be a narrative process that we will start from the beginning of the meditation process and walk through together. Often when doing processes with an individual in session or energy exercises in a class, we will describe the whole process before engaging. This is the approach we'll take in this chapter and on into the descriptions of the elements of the Great Hall of Records.

So as we start our process of preparing to journey we may get a glass of water. Lighting a candle may be a helpful element, I prefer a white candle. Next we do whatever relaxing energizing meditation, breathing or energy exercise that we feel works best for us before our Akashic journey. As we then find a comfortable place to relax, maybe it's an easy chair, recliner, the couch or even lying down in bed.

As you begin to breathe in the cosmic pranic energy into the chakra center(s) that best work for you in your process (we'll indicate more of these in the journey exercise sections) You may now sequentially be experiencing sensations in the chakras, the eyes, the brain, and/or different areas of your body and energy fields.

This allows you to start tending yourself into your guided journey with the colorful imagery that you've chosen for this Akashic meditation exercise. There are multiple ways in which we journey up and out of the body to get into the Records. Sometimes we journey up and out of the chest and face. Sometimes we journey up and out through the crown chakra or the 3rd eye brow center. Sometimes we journey simply from the guided imagery itself up and out. So as we tend up and out we are still connected with the physical body. We are here and there at the same time as we project and expand our fields simultaneously. As we journey up to the outer atmospheres where there is no electromagnetic interference. As we move up outside of the earth's field we connect with the energy of the sun which is a very powerful and uplifting thing to do.

As we then slip into our colorful guided imagery journey and into the setting(s) that will take us into the Akashic Records Hall location. We generally use an outdoor setting or a stream of Divine Light to start out the transitional flight. As we move in whatever way the journey takes us and delivers us to the Great Hall of Records, we arrive there before the doors of a great temple.

The archetypical images will start to emanate energy the more we start to go into the whole vision. Next we find the great ancient doors in front of the temple. Often times there will be lions on either side of the doors protecting it. This is a subconscious prompt that activates your inner awareness and alertness while also continuing to remain calm. Imagine if you were in front of two very real lions! Even if they were relaxed and you were relaxed you would probably feel some unusual sensations about being in their presence. Your empathic field in the real world would be immediately activated and expanded.

The outside of the structure will have an interesting detail for you depending on how you interpret the energy and how your mind channels it into imagery. It can feel and look ancient, It can feel and look artistic or divinely heaven-like. Let it unfold uniquely for You.

The inside of the hall has unique qualities. One thing you might notice immediately or over time is that the walls and/or ceiling can seem to be transparent or semi-transparent. The structure itself may be composed of energetic spatial geometries or may resemble ancient architecture of stone or wood. As you are in the realm of the Records here, there are many dynamic objects, energy sources and objective/subjective forms of **oracles** that can appear for you to work with. Oracles pertain to objects or sources of messages, energy and information.

This can include a massive book on a table or altar. There may appear to be scrolls also. The room often appears to be like a great library to many people who visit. Walls and shelves full of books or scrolls that either the visitor, the librarian or a guide may access in order to convey certain information or messages. There may be tapestries that also convey and contain images and information. Often times these are moving with energy. There can be any number of angels, guides, family members or the Keepers of the Records that can appear to bring messages or healing for a visitor to the Records. Also there can be any number of objects from other lifetimes that can materialize or be presented to a person that will have a connection mentally for that individual back to another lifetime.

We will be using several different ways to access, approach, experience and move up into and through the Records. We'll also take different meditation and visualization approaches to get into the Akasha which will have different mental approaches within the subtle mental body of your experiences.

So in summary there are many elements that we will be exploring in more detail in the following sections that will bring life to the actual process of colorfully accessing and entering into a successful **Akashic Records Journey Experience**. See you in the Records!

Welcome to the Akashic Records

Chapter 2
The Tapestry of Souls

*W*ithin the realms of the higher dimensions the energy of time and space is operating much differently than it does here on planet earth at this time. This may be a relatively different comparison of energetics if you are reading this well into the future as the energy here on earth will continue to shift. It may also be different if you're reading this in space, on a ship or another planet. Maybe you're reading from a floating city of the future or deep within the planet.

There will be a resurgence or a rekindling of connecting with one's personal Soul records as we travel forward in time. As the energy continues to shift it will be easier and easier in many ways to connect in with your Soul Records and your personal

Book of Life. It will be easier to have incarnations here and the conflicts will be much less in many ways. The word 'conflict' here refers to different levels and forms of conflicting energies. There will be more of an ease in the pressures of atmospheric duality. This is often what we experience now in the current day and age when we are meditating and feeling blissful. When this happens we are connected with nature and outside the reach of our day to day or moment to moment reactions to stress and tension from all of life's challenges.

We are talking about a very light feeling. How long has it been since you've felt a really light and clear feeling? I remember once going and going for long periods of time earlier in my life from day to day with work and play as all of the colorful things in a persons life that keep us jumping through hoops.

Until one day I had a memorable moment that stuck with me. As I stopped in the middle of my art studio, I could here the street traffic faintly in the background and I was looking at a table fan that was blowing. For a moment the blades seemed to stop or slow down. In this timeless moment it didn't matter that the blades could even have been going in the other direction. In fact it looked as if they were and in that moment, I wasn't sure. There was a peaceful field of energy that expanded and as it did, time seemed to stop. As the setting sun came in through the windows and shown across the wall. There was a peace that seemed to make time stand still and seemed much longer than it was.

This was a contrasting moment to the rest of daily reality. This is the kind of peace I'm talking about. The kind of peace and/or high vibration that the ones who we refer to as masters experience all the time. This is an everyday experience for them from moment to moment. This is what we have to look forward to.

Like that timeless 'Now; moment streaming more and more timelessly in the coming future. Why wait for evolution and the future when we can start now? The focus here is this peaceful timeless moment in comparison to the rest of normal day to day time & space reality operating here in the normal throws of society. Here in the 'real' world so to speak if dare call it that.

Where are we going with all this? This reality, the 3rd dimension has other dimensions one after another, one on top of another, one within another, depending on how you perspectively look at it, grasp for an understanding of it or wrap your mind around it. The coinciding other dimensions such as 4th, 5th, 6th, 7th, 8th, 9th & 10th and so on, all have there own energy dynamics. Each one somewhat lighter and higher in vibration than the previous.

So as we step up into the Akasha or sky library and the place of the Great Temple of the Akashic Records. Here in the higher dimensions, this place is visited continually by the Souls of humanity between lifetimes and those coming to earth for the first time. This Hall is also visited by the Great Masters of humanity, the Ascended Masters and the Arc Angels of the Light. As we come up through the dimensions from incarnations on earth in between lifetimes, all the Souls come to look into their Book of Life to see what they have learned or what has been healed and what is next for the Soul's journey.

As the Souls visit the Akashic Records so do the masters, teachers, healers, and angels coming to be guides for these Souls as well as for healing with others still on earth or still within an existing incarnational body as well as Souls out of body.

As we continue to journey into the Records we may find many master teachers and healers there. It may also be an isolated visit to our own experience so as we are not distracted as to why we're there. Often others report to have had experiences with being in a great library or a classroom type of a setting. This is the Akashic Records.

Within the Great Hall and in the higher dimensions which operate much differently than this dimension, there is a Great Tapestry. A tapestry woven from the Light of all Souls of Humanity and beyond that are visiting the earth plane through incarnations. This may also include Souls that are in the world physically and in the atmosphere between lives.

This tapestry is a flow chart or colorful mapping

diagram fully alive with all of the colors of light that we know and even colors we do not have here in our spectrum. How amazing all of this is to look into once you view or arrive into the Akashic Records and you're actually looking past the dream vision into the higher dimensional reality of what actually exists there.

This will always play a definitive role with interpreting your visionary work. Having to sort out what's been colorfully depicted in the metaphysical arena with all of it's many facets and descriptions over time. There will always be a curve as to how we're directing the metaphysical matrix in our work with the energetic and imaginative variations and how that is in comparison to what actually exists in the higher realms. This refers to our filters and how clear they are.

This **Tapestry of Souls** is so energetically unique that you can look into it, view into it, continually and get uniquely directed information about individual paths, incarnations or any number of other topics concerning the group consciousness of humanity and how it dances through all of the Souls.

Two modern day movie references that remind me in a somewhat similar way: 1. In the Xmen Charles Xavier (Professor X) connects with his machine called 'Cerebro'. It allows him to find individuals in the world or to connect with the whole of humanity. For the greater good.

2: Thor: The Keeper of the Rainbow bridge that

beams them down to earth and to other places. As he looks down to earth from Asgard, the Nordic Realm, he can see what's happening here on earth and even in individuals' lives even as he is light years away in higher dimensions. These are science fiction references though it's a similar reference as looking into the Tapestry of Souls.

Tapestries throughout earth history have symbolized the social elements of the cultures they were created by. Social castes and status were often represented by certain colors, weaves and symbols. Certain religious rites often required certain tapestries, shawls, or clothing.

Designs were often specific to family groups, royal families and even militaries. Some cultures were known for making war rugs which had symbolic and wishful ritualistic references of a coming war, fight or conflict with another country and were woven in a hopeful favor of their victory. Rugs, tapestries and garments were often also used as a form of trade or currency.

So weaving began at it's earliest stages as an art form which was also crafted for it's purposeful need. Much like the wheel and other classic simple cornerstone designs which we rely heavily on in today's world without giving it much thought. These were no small inventions when they were born. These were things that changed the world.

And when the tapestries were first crafted it was

all about the thoughtfulness going into the finished product. Often there were prayers or songs that were chanted, blessing the woven tapestries and other forms giving them a special vibration. Throughout history in many parts of the world and even today the traditional arts of weaving sacred cloths and fabrics is still practiced.

So while we look into the higher dimensions and the Akashic Records to this Tapestry of Souls, could it be that the tapestries of this world and the practice of making them was somehow linked to the Great Tapestry in the Hall of Records? Has the energy translated or stepped down to the earth plane from the higher dimensions of the Records through the creative vibrations of the Souls incarnating on earth and creating continually as we humans are known to do? This is something to consider as all of the many creations and inventions here on earth were born from the same Akashic energy and the higher mind stepping down into reality.

Creator God and the higher vibrational angelics associated with creation itself had participated in weaving or creating a Great Tapestry of Souls which hangs in the main Hall of Records where the keepers, guides and teachers work with the Souls who are busy coming and going through the process of incarnation. A very large rainbow colored tapestry that shows the trends and the migrations of Soul groups. Showing the different levels of Soul groups as the tapestry is alive with the collective energy of all the Souls. Could this be compared to the schedules in Grand Central Station or in airports?

These are the workings of the higher dimensions. There the ideas of space and time and of length, width and height have a unique quality. As you're in the higher dimensions you will notice these dynamics of space time qualities as being simultaneously and interactively different.

You may notice that there is no distance between moments in the Eternal Now as everything is happening simultaneously and yet it can seem to be happening over the course of great expanses of experiential moments. No distance, no time. All distance, all time.

Objects can appear to have shape and color and yet no real density. Things can appear to be very spacial and yet they can also appear to have a sort of 2 dimensional resemblance while also taking on the streaming qualities that morph into the higher dimensions. These are the qualities of space time dimensional reality that we're dealing with when you're in the Akashic Records Hall first hand and when you're viewing the Great Tapestry of Souls in person. And as you continue your Journeys into the Akashic Records you'll understand and experience more about how the energy moves with you as you look into the Great Tapestry, your Book of Life and other aspects of the higher dimensions.

LET'S VIEW THE GREAT TAPESTRY OF SOULS WITHIN THE AKASHIC RECORDS
Read the Script
and then practice your self guided visualization.

As you start to relax finding a comfortable place to lay down or sit. Just continue to breathe in and out slowly, deeply and gently. Let go of all of your cares and concerns of the day. As you continue to breathe, visualize your chakras clear and evenly balanced. Visualize a Great Hall peaceful and quiet like a library and stay in this energy of the library. It is very soft and subtle peace and quiet. As you visualize with your mind, See now a great tapestry before you now in the Hall.

This Tapestry is full of Light. It contains every color in the known spectrum, every shade and variation. It also has colors that are unknown in our color palette of the 3D spectrum. The Tapestry is like a great living diagram and flow chart of all of the Souls who have ever visited the earth plane through the Akasha and all of the Souls who are now incarnate and connected through their Books of Life. Just take a few moments to view and to connect with the energy of the Tapestry. You are connecting into the Library of Souls, The Tapestry of Souls and your place within it all as you take a few moments to visit within this place and space. Having connected with the Great Tapestry of Souls let's come back to the Here and Now, coming back to the room. Welcome yourself back fully into your body.

Chapter 3
Windows to the Cosmos

There are many ways to creatively and perspectively view into the Akashic Records and the Akashic Hall of Wisdom. As you look in through your mind's eye (your 3rd eye) we journey up through the sky through the 5th dimension or the astral plane and then onward up through consecutive dimensions until we reach our destination, the Great Hall of Records.

As we come into the Great Hall there are many nuances that we are taking in with our senses. As you continue to look around at all of the decor notice the details. As you feel into the essence of where you have landed. The cosmic energy is emanating through this place. The vibrations are very subtle though they carry the frequency of not only the great library of this planet, but also of heaven and the frequencies of the stars systems as well.

As you move spatially through this Great Hall

and you are within the higher dimensions which have their own unique perspectives, notice the size of the great hall and notice the way you feel in this room. You may be experiencing a certain level of freedom that you were not previously accustomed to. Feel the ability in your inner self as you are participating here in your dream vision to move about very easily and to expand in a spacious manner.

Like an energetic breath of fresh air. A deep, peaceful and easy feeling within and around you. Is this feeling more of what you would like to bring into your physical life? There is a natural translation of energy between the two worlds. The more you visit this peaceful and reverent space, the more it will bring it's subtle emanations down through your soul which will then translate into your physical body, mind, chakras and senses and finally out into your world from You. It will help You to transform yourself in ways as you now intend subtle and dynamic levels of change by starting this process.

Even if you only experienced it once. That peaceful vibration of heaven and of the Records is enough for you to remember energetically and tend yourself back to whether it's within days, months or years. Your Soul will not forget the way and the connection. It will lead you back, if not consciously, then in dreams. Often times when we need to see, experience or understand something in our lives that we cannot seem to grasp a hold of in any other way for whatever reasons, it will often find us and present itself to us in our dreams.

So in finding the Great Hall and moving about it freely whether in guided intended meditations or through dreaming, the experience is that of being in a place of surroundings that are much bigger and make you feel much greater than you may feel in your day to day moment to moment reality.

Within this place you may start to experience the feelings of weightlessness, like every movement is effortless.

You may experience the reference of timelessness. When the past, present and future all merge together within the streaming Eternal Now Moment.

You may experience a release, loss, or absence of any dark or negative feelings or emotions within your mind, body and spirit that may have been with you for a long time. They are just gone. They are not part of you when you're within this space, and there is a very light happy feeling that replaces it. Let's call this joy, love or bliss. This possible experience alone is enough to lead you back into the Akashic Records again. It just feels good to be there.

This can be the place for many where the pain, suffering, fears and traumas are released and just gone or lifted. We have had experiences of going back repetitively in our lives and reliving the pain over & over or time looping if you will, and why? What's the pay off that we receive in doing this? Is it the continued security of familiar levels of stress, that lead us back to denser and lower vibrational living?

Back to the Great Hall of Records. So with all the timeless, weightless, streaming energy sensations from within the Records, the higher dimensions are vibrating or flickering at a higher and lighter rate. The divine structure of the Hall itself can often appear to be transparent or semi-transparent. As you visit the Great Hall of Records you may notice that the ceiling is transparent or the walls are giving way to eternity.

You may see outer space or you may see eternity. Or both. You may witness that as the walls, ceiling and even the floor somewhat fall away, they are still held in integrity of the space and place which you are visiting. The Akashic Records in many ways will have a very heavenly feel to it. You will remember it as being very heaven-like.

The transparency of the walls and/or ceiling and floor we will use from time to time in our journeys into the Records. For instance, we may be in the Great Hall and we may be connecting through a pillar of Light that goes up through the ceiling and into the Source Light of Creation. As we do this the ceiling may seem to become or already having the quality of transparency. In the higher dimensions it is that you see the surface of things and you look through them and you look beyond them all at the same time.

The same can be true with the walls and floors. You may see them and be looking at them and spatially moving beyond them all at the same time. Looking out across space and time into eternity. You may experience looking down at the world through the floor. You are experiencing multiple perspectives simultaneously. You are looking at it, through it and beyond it all at the same time. ('it' meaning any object)

The colors of the higher dimensions are going to have a different look also. They may translate as the same colors as here on Earth in 3 dimensional reality so that you can have a more beneficial experience. Though in truth the higher dimensions including the Akashic Records can have a very different color spectrum. The colors may actually seem to have textures to them or sometimes a sound vibration, an emotion or even a certain flavor.

So let's suppose you are looking up at the ceiling in the Great Hall of Records. You may see a very high ceiling with archways that give you the sense of expansion. In this sense you may be experiencing a more conventional color palate. If you start to shift into more of a high vibrational state through your soul, mind and your senses, you might experience the transparencies that we were previously describing.

This 'see-through' transparent effect causes different lighting and color variations to occur. You may see the ceiling as more of very translucent light greys or what could also be described as more of an absence of color. You could also see the ceiling shifting through different color spectrums causing a changing and shifting sensory movie to occur. This will give you the feeling that the room is alive with energy which is actually true.

Now the same dynamic can happen with the walls of the Great Hall as well. The same transparent effect causing your perspective to shift from opaque to translucent and shades or levels of perception in between. Think of Clark Kent in the Superman movies with his X-Ray vision. Remember to the scenes where he is learning to use his gift of second sight. His vision and the energy is adjusting and causing him to see at different varied X-ray levels.

In the Ancestral Healing Process we utilize a grand picture window right at the other end of the Hall. Through this window we see the center of the Universe. The Source Light of All Creation. Many would refer to this as God. It is millions of light years away in our waking state. Here in the Hall of Records through this Window to Eternity the visual distance appears to be far and yet somehow local at the same time. It is far enough away to appear distant and yet is just close enough to give us that grandiose sensation, like being in front of the Grand Canyon. This is a very unique dynamic, and another example of what we were sharing earlier in the chapter about time, space and distance.

So when your energy and perception is expanding more the walls and ceiling can become translucent to completely transparent. When your energy and focus is concentrated everything may have the illusion of seeming like there are solids or boundaries. Enjoy working with this dynamic. In the grand scheme of things you will be using this perspective quite a lot in the Akashic Records and then bringing that perspective into your senses here in the physical reality is also quite possible.

As you look along each side of the Great Hall you may see arched stained glass windows which are very long and tall. They represent and are truly windows to the cosmos as the cosmic starlight of the Universe, the higher worlds and of Eternity come streaming through the great windows. The stained glass is made of many colors.

Brightly colored panes which are comprised of many different shapes and sizes. Some of the shapes are larger, some mid-sized and some smaller. They are all varying sizes and make up the whole of the great window panes. Much like all the elements that make up our world are part of the oneness of the Uni-verse. Everything is connected.

While the colored glass pieces in the window frame are different variations of all shapes and sizes, they are all joined together through the window to make up the whole. And then light is shining through them all together creating a symphony of tones and light. The other worldly quality to the windows causes the patterns of the colors to gently move with energy. Because they are alive in this place with the **Divine Intelligence** that moves through all things.

The grace of Heaven shines through these portals. With great intensity of even streams of flowing light from the Great Light of the Central Sun and the star systems that are all connected as a network beaming through into the Great Hall. As the cosmic energy shines through the colored glass it creates colored beams of light that shine down onto the floor. The whole creative dynamic of this place within the higher dimensions is quite remarkable to behold.

Let's View the Windows of the Cosmos Within the Akashic Records
*Read the Script
and then practice your self guided visualization.*

As you start to relax finding a comfortable place to lay down or sit. Just continue to breathe in and out slowly, deeply and gently. Let go of all of your cares and concerns of the day. As you continue to breathe, visualize your chakras clear and evenly balanced. Visualize a Great Hall peaceful and quiet like a library and stay in this energy of the library. The soft and subtle peace and quiet. As you visualize with your mind, See and travel by thought to the Hall.

Windows to the Cosmos

As you enter in through the front doors, you look around at the very spacious high ceilings and tall walls. Feel the spaciousness of this room. Notice the very high arched ceiling. The ceiling and the walls are semi-transparent and you can see through them across outer space or through and into different dimensions. There are very tall stained glass windows lining each side of the hall. See them now all in a row on each side of the hall.

Windows to the Cosmos. Great beams of colored light are shining down through the windows, as they shine across the floor in colored patterns. See the streams of colored light beaming across the hall. Notice how the colored light creates patterns across the floor. Just take a few moments to be in the moment of the Great Hall with it's walls, arched ceilings and tall stained glass windows. And when you're ready just come back to the Here and Now in this moment. Welcome Home.

Chapter 4
The Mosaic Floor

The more that you continue to do this work and look into the other side, the higher dimensions and the Akashic Records, you begin to gain a more holographic sense of all things spiritual or that which is unseen. The Latin term 'spirit' originally meant 'breath' or 'breath of God'.

You start to open more to the inner workings of the mind's eye. You start to perceive and to see in very subtle, colorful, and clearer ways into the other side or the unseen. The 'unseen' can be a very large category and I like to refer to it largely as the workings of the astral plane. Many if not most of us have had psychic notions and moments of perception that we could not explain but which seem to be very natural or organic.

When we are having these naturally organic psychic moments, perceptions or dreams, we usually are utilizing the 5th dimensional energy through the mind's eye. The properties of 5th dimension are easily utilized by the human mind and also utilizes the 4th dimension primarily as constructs of the mind and thought. For most people here in 3rd Dimension reality, they are unconsciously aware of the vast multitude of dimensions that the human mind has access to. While the 5th Dimension world is closer to the mind's play ground than the other dimensions, the mind makes this jump easily and can connect us in through our senses, our dreams, our body, our thoughts and also via psychic awareness.

So as you become more fluent with seeing natural or organic impressions in your mind, you will be seeing naturally animated energy. Colorful snapshots and instantaneous pictures that can seem very crisp. You will come to know when the pictures, flashes and visions are from Spirit, the Higher Realms and/or the Akashic Records. They will have a certain feel, a certain look and energy that you can't mistake as subtle as it may be.

In the last chapter we talked about the transparency of forms in the higher dimensions. The walls and the ceilings of the Akashic Hall of Wisdom. You may also have flashes in other ways such as looking into the tissue of someone's physical body or into your own body for the purpose of messages concerning healing.

So in the same fashion as the surfaces becoming transparent within the higher dimensions, they can also become animated. As we now turn our attention to the floors of the Great Hall. As we're travelling up in our Akashic Records journeys and you come to the Great Hall most often we enter in through the front doors just as we normally would. As we step into the Great Hall the spatial perspective and the energy of the place are the first two things that we perceive. The wide open feel of the amazing floor. What does the floor look like to you at first glance if you were to have had no outside influences in your study of it?

In our journeys and since times memorial, the ancients have reported that certain elements of the building itself seem to be alive or animated with energy and also with information. These are the elements of perfecting the creative intuitive arts.

As we've spoken about in other volumes of information, there are archetypes of form which have been focused upon by groups and individuals over the course of history by human mystics within the Akashic Records. These forms after being creatively focused on for so long in mystical meditation techniques are found to be imprinted in the higher dimensions in this etheric and highly protected Temple of the Souls.

There are also elements and features of this Great Hall of the Akashic Records here in this Temple of Souls that are part of it's original creation of it. Sometimes the features are easily seen and worked with and sometimes they are transformed or converted into simpler archetypical forms, features and elements that can be more readily worked with by the human mind.

The great expansive floors are lined with mosaic tiles which are animated and reanimated with information, knowledge and wisdom. As you step into the Hall, a Great Light shines down upon you. As you walk through the colors of each chakra bathing your being in the light. The lights expose the mosaics and mandalas that are living and breathing with energy. Much like it is said that all forms of creation emanate from the Sri Yantra and the Flower of Life Mandalas, the mosaics of the Great Temple store and breathe with the same essence of creation in it's own special way.

And as you walk across these living mosaics, you are coming into direct contact with the foundation of this system of information. The Great Divine Floor Plan if you will of galactic creation pertaining to this planet, Gaia or as we call her, Mother Earth. This living mosaic floor is a direct indication that not only the information from within the Records is continually perpetuating but also the Records themselves are unfolding collectively, as is our own personal Book of Life.

As you go through your life, details of your physical reality are translated into the Records and becomes imprinted in your Book. So it is being written for you, about you and by you. All of the streaming information which you may have access to later by remembering to these translated imprints that you may now read through and become more connected and aware. There is an added level of what we will call '**creative entanglement**'. A deeper connection experienced when we intend directly back into the source of our Soul Records. Which will in turn have the options to affect our living time space reality from our own point of reference within it.

Let's View the Mosaic Floor Within the Akashic Records
Read the Script
and then practice your self guided visualization.

As you start to relax finding a comfortable place to lay down or sit. Just continue to breathe in and out slowly, deeply and gently. Let go of all of your cares and concerns of the day. As you continue to breathe, visualize your chakras clear and evenly balanced.

Visualize a Great Hall peaceful and quiet like a library and stay in this energy of the library. The soft and subtle peace and quiet. As you visualize with your mind, See and travel by thought to the Hall. As you enter in through the front doors, you look around at the very spacious high ceilings and tall walls.

Feel the spaciousness of this room. Notice the very high arched ceiling. The ceiling and the walls are semi-transparent and you can see through them across outer space or through and into different dimensions. There are stained glass windows lining each side of the hall.

Great beams of colored light are shining down

through the windows, as they shine across the floor in colored patterns. As you're standing there, you look down at the floor that you now walk across. So open and spacious. Look at the tiles and look at the detail of the tiles. There are mosaics on the floor tiles that are moving with energy. Look at the patterns of the mosaics. Geometric shapes and patterns, fractals, mandalas. and sacred symbols.

What do the patterns and shapes look like? Are they moving with energy? What are the thoughts and feelings that you get from the mosaics? Are you receiving messages as you walk across this great floor?

Just take a few moments to be in the moment of the Great Hall with it's walls, arched ceilings, tall stained glass windows and mosaic floors. And when you're ready just come back to the Here and Now in this moment. Welcome Home.

The Mosaic Floor

Chapter 5

THE BOOK OF LIFE

So many of the little things in life we can easily take for granted. Riding a bicycle or saying hello to someone. Reading a book or newspaper or simply walking across the street. It is always good for us to be grateful, kind, loving and thoughtful towards all things in life. As we think about our lives and all of the many functions and objects that we use throughout the day.

One of the things that we use in everyday life is a book. For everything from training and learning to entertainment and reference or the arts. Books are important in our lives. As a culture they keep us reading and writing. Creating from our imaginations and being inventive. Seeing everything written and illustrated, printed and published. In our world we like to collect these books as much as we like to create them. Books are full of our culture, knowledge, creativity and entertainment.

All of the great philosophers, story tellers, poets and researchers have all contributed great writings which were transcribed onto scrolls and then later into books. There are many ancient writings that did not make it into being translated as a book. So many ancient documents were lost. Never to be seen again.

This is one reason why accessing the Akashic Records can be important for historical referencing. The more we practice it, we can have access to ancient civilizations and parts of history that have been lost in the mist. There is much to see from within the Records. So many millions of years, ages upon ages. What will your vision be like? The rise and fall of different cultures and races. Great events that shaped the face of the world.

All of the great scholars, teachers, healers, leaders, humanitarians, artists, builders and the list goes on. What will your interpretation be? Great libraries built in different parts of the world including the Library of Alexandria, Egypt. The concept and construction of a place of great knowledge, a collection of books and scrolls. Did we transpose this idea from the Great Hall of Records itself?

My thoughts, questions, inquiries and ideas here are that we may be downloading and building that which already exists in the higher dimensions. Temples, books, scrolls, tapestries, art forms, geometries. As we started to craft our civilization it has been said that Necessity is the Mother of all

Invention. It could be a blend of these two origins of channelled creation. From the ethers of the higher forms and from our own needs in the moment to navigate our reality more gracefully.

You will get a sense of what came from above and what was created on the earth plane from the mind of humanity as your journeys into the Akashic Records continue. You have much to look forward to in your investigations and inquiries into the Great Sky Library.

Before you go into those great banks of knowledge, it is best to master entry into your own Book of Life or Book of Lifetimes. Much of *Vol. 1 New Beginnings* was about entry into your Book. Once you have found your way into your own personal records then and only then is it a good idea to investigate the rest of the library. It will be much easier for you if you start with your own Soul's Records first. This is the key reason the Akasha exists. For You to study *your* Records.

Again this is the wide, wide world of the Akashic Records so let's keep it simple and start in a systematic and creatively productive manner. The generator of all of your personal experiences here on planet Earth in this lifetime is your Book of Life. You're writing in it as you have experiences simultaneously. You with your guides and the Keeper of the Records all decided between lives, before you came to the Earth plane with agreements of the lessons and experiences that you wanted to have in this lifetime.

Your Book of Life is your personal gateway into your own self knowledge. Everyone here in human form has an etheric book stored in the Records or in 'heaven'. As we describe it here, familiarize yourself with it and continually practice your own meditations into your personal Book within the Records. By doing this you are cultivating self knowledge.

The archetype of the Book itself symbolizes the collection of chapters representing your incarnations or lifetimes in a multi-dimensional and non-linear perspective. Life events, of which you will have situational responses to, and a collection of lifetimes of your Celestial Soul and your Body Spirit.

The Celestial Souls as part of God coming from the center of creation are born of other stars or progressively visiting from other civilizations among the stars. The Body Spirit is the Soul portion of the physical body which contains the memories of all the lifetimes on this planet here within the current family bloodline, other families of the same race or other races. These two parts of a person's **Celestial Soul** and **Body Spirit** make up the detailed information that is written in your Book of Life.

The Book of Lifetimes also contains codes for healing and ascension. As you connect with your Book you have major intuitive, Soul based integration, healing and karmic repair that starts happening for you. The symbols are light based frequency codes that resonate with you in the best integrative pattern for your vibration. As you continue to visit your Book it continues to work with you.

We have recommended first viewing into your own Book of Lifetimes before going into the whole spectrum of the Records. Though, in your inquiries, you will be viewing, seeing and visiting other lifetimes and other places where you have been in the Universe and possibly other dimensions which will show you details of other time periods, feelings and sensations. You will gain much knowledge from other places and the details surrounding those incarnations.

This is all assimilated by the mind so that you can reconnect, revisit, remember the pathways to those times and places for further experiences and journeys to help explore a wider range of information such as historical events or the details of a well known person in history perhaps associated with the world's progress.

As we come in through the front doors of the Akashic Hall of Records, we see the arched ceilings and the windows lining the hall. As you look to the other end we see a classic version of a very large and old wooden table. An altar of sorts. And on this altar there is a Book, a very large book shining softly and emitting a glow of energy which is your soul energy.

As you approach the Book either by walking over to it or being immediately transported in front of it, the Great Book has a presence which is living and breathing because it is part of You. You can feel it's presence. It is somewhat like looking in the mirror. And as you're pulled to this mirror the energy is heightened as you sense it, feel it and resonate with it.

The pages can turn by themselves for you or you can manually flip through them. They send you to different areas of the book, sections and chapters where there is work to be done. The book has writings within it that your Soul has placed there as you change, ebb and flow, learn and grow, heal, release and create anew in your life.

Whatever the case may be, the passages and groups of writings and symbols can change, transform and re-pattern themselves for you so that you can live your life in a way that best suits you. In this inner circle of re-patterning or restructuring life events, when you are looking directly at it and you see it for what it is, you are changing and in so doing reorganizing the book. It's like a self auto-correct that always works to your best benefit and favor.

There can appear at times the detail of very tall transparent glass like dividers appearing around the altar and Book of Life that are glowing with a faint blue. This is like a baffle or barrier while you are in your own records which isolates the rest of the Hall, while you are focused directly down into the Book. Within the faint blue glowing glass, there are symbols appearing and moving horizontally and vertically, some slower and some faster.

Although when you are in the Records you may see slight or dramatic variations on this theme. There is a frequency that runs down the blue transparent glass panes like a water flowing continuously. This helps to give life to the patterns of symbols coming in from creation.

Let's View the Book of Life Within the Akashic Records
*Read the Script
and then practice your self guided visualization.*

As you start to relax finding a comfortable place to lay down or sit. Just continue to breathe in and out slowly, deeply and gently. Let go of all of your cares and concerns of the day. As you continue to breathe, visualize your chakras clear and evenly balanced. Visualize a Great Hall peaceful and quiet like a library and stay in this energy of the library. The soft and subtle peace and quiet.

As you visualize with your mind, See and travel by thought to the Hall. As you enter in through the front doors, you look around at the very spacious high ceilings and tall walls. Feel the spaciousness of this room. Notice the very high arched ceiling. The ceiling and the walls are semi-transparent and you can see through them across outer space or through and into different dimensions.

There are stained glass windows lining each side of the hall. Great beams of colored light are shining down through the windows, as they shine across the floor in colored patterns. As you're standing there you look down at the floor that you now walk across. So open and spacious. Look at the tiles and look at the detail of the tiles. There are mosaics on the floor tiles that are moving with energy. Look at the patterns of the mosaics. Geometric shapes and patterns, fractals, mandalas and sacred symbols. Just take a few moments to be in the moment of the Great Hall with it's walls, arched ceilings, tall stained glass windows and mosaic floors. As you now look to the other end of the Hall, you see a very large and old table like an altar.

On this ancient altar is a very large book. Your Book of Life. As you walk over to the book across the mosaic patterns on the floor, You stand before your very own personal story of your Soul's journey. Just take a few moments to familiarize yourself with your Soul Records. Look at the Book and it's physical/etheric details and nuances. As you look into the Book notice that it's open to your current lifetime. Spend some time with the book and it's connection to You and your Soul... And when you're ready just come back to the Here and Now in this moment. Welcome Home.

The Book of Life

Chapter 6

THE MYSTICAL MIRROR

OF THE AKASHA

The Akashic Records as a you can see at this point has many different nuances and components to work with. This interactive collection of information is quite different than anything else in our known universe. The different Halls of Records for each planet and celestial bodies with their own special keepers, are one of the most unique systems that you will find anywhere. The interactive intuitive elements within the Great Hall that we've mentioned so far are all very distinct in their functions and placement within this grand library.

As we look into the Akasha through the great oracle available to us here, we are utilizing our brain and the coinciding mind field, the 3rd eye and crown chakra, the rest of the chakra system along the spinal column, our empathic field and our soul's intuition field. It's pretty amazing that we have so many parts of ourselves that we actually use intuitively and psychically. As we journey up into the higher dimensions, passing through the astral plane and on up into the higher finer energies in the outer reaches of Earth's atmosphere where the energy is high and clear. We isolate the senses as we journey out of the face, chest and crown through a guided journey portal and on up into the Akashic Records.

The process utilizes your inner vision or your **Akashic Vision**. As you utilize this inner vision, you activate certain regions of the brain and energy centers including the eyes. You activate your crown chakra coming from the pineal gland in the center of the brain. You activate your 3rd eye or brow center coming from the pituitary gland sitting in the center of the head in front of the pineal gland just under the frontal lobes of the brain in a small intricate bone casing.

As you activate the 3rd Eye you also utilize the optical eyes. All three of the eyes actually work together as a team. This amplifies the inner vision psychic signal and energy. As the optical eyes are activated the energy travels in and out simultaneously through the eyes and then through the optical nerves which connect into the brain and into the neocortex or the vision centers in the back of the brain. This is where the vision of sight and of dreams are experienced.

The vision centers of the brain that are experienced

in connection to bringing in sensory input from the 3D physical world, visual input from dreams, images from the subconscious mind and the super conscious mind, and visionary and visual imprints from psychic visions including intuitive or Akashic Records inquiries associated with the Soul energy and the higher dimensions.

The brain utilizes the thought process through the vehicle of the mind field. Have you ever wondered where thoughts come from? In ancient times when the energy was very different and very subtle, the study of energy flow in the body was important to the physical, mental and energy science of health.

The ancients had arrived that thought forms or certain levels of vibration enter in through the left eye and then are sent out. Certain levels of vibration and thought projections go out through the right eye. We also utilize both left and right optical eyes for sending or projecting and also for receiving messages and input from our surroundings on all levels. So you can imagine that there is a very intricate firing of energy back and forth through the left and right sides of the brain and the body, the left and right eyes, the spinal fluid, and other regions or centers of the body all simultaneously.

As the eyes utilize the bands of energy that are entering into the mind field from the local and long range ethers, the mind then uses those frequencies and energy to pattern certain thoughts based on a person's own personal collection of lifetime stories and images. There's always an emotional or subconscious connection to other things that we've already experienced, until a person is ready to change and to rewrite old thought programs. So the mind field is a very busy place with the mechanics of consciousness moving through the eyes, the chakras, the brain and the mind field. As you go about your momentary, continual and creative every day thought processes, think about the dynamics of these intricate energy workings. This may give you more insight and quite a different look as to what's been going on inside your brain and mind all these years. This working model gives us many reasons to fine tune our thinking process.

Drinking plenty of water is important as the mind system and body's energy system runs on **hydroelectricity**. Salt, minerals and electrolytes are also important for this process as are Amino acids, peptides and proteins for the brain.

Get out to nature and off the grid if possible to connect with the earth, sky, trees and water such as a lake, river, stream or the ocean. Sitting in the grass with your back up against a tree can be very clearing and grounding. Connecting with nature helps you to release energy from the electromagnetic frequency waves of energy or **EMF** that we are continually bombarded with in the cities and our homes from appliances, cell phones and the internet. Getting out to nature can really give your body and your mind a rest. It may also help you to understand that you may want to gauge or limit your energy device usage.

Meditate and exercise. Sitting stationary and relaxing your mind while breathing can be very freeing. And exercise can also be very clearing as you are really moving the energy through your body. This is really good for you and it will help to free and release old stuck energies in the body, mind and spirit as well as keep you burning those calories and extra fat as you build muscle tissue. In today's world we have many demands but we can still take good care of ourselves even if it's as simple as eating an apple, drinking a glass of water and going for a walk. Keep it simple.

Watch your food intake. Limit your snacks between meals and eating too late in the day. Limiting your grain input or stopping grains all together can be very helpful. Often times gluten free products are helpful, though many people still have secondary inflammation in the body tissue caused by grains and sugars. Juice and a good source of filtered water are your friends.

Cleansing from time to time can also bring amazing mental clarity. When we cleanse, if done correctly, we need to change our diet to a cleaner regiment. A colon cleanse is always a good place to start. Kidney and bladder next followed by liver and gal bladder. Cleansing in moderation will help you to bring in sharper and clearer mental imagery and visions. Always consult a qualified source before starting any cleanse processes to make sure your doing it safely.

Now as we move back into the Records, we find the Tapestry of Souls. We find the mosaic floor and the cosmic translucent walls and ceiling. As we look to the far end of the hall adjacent to the front doors, we see a very ancient table or an old wooden altar. Hand carved and very decorative with ancient woods. As you move your awareness across the room to the ancient altar, we now see a very large and ancient book, your Book of Life. We went into detail with the Book of life in Vol. 1 but let's revisit here for a moment. The Book of Life with the Akashic Hall of Wisdom in many ways is your focal point for bringing in information.

All of the chapters of your lifetimes are here within your book. Past, Present, and even Future impressions are available for your inquiries. The book is emanating with energy...your energy. The same energy we will discuss in the Rooms and Sections chapter. Your energy radiating from the book is your Soul energy. When you come into contact and connect with the book you are looking directly into your own Soul energy. This is an important connection in that it strengthens your connection to not only your own Records within the Akasha, the Akashic Records in general, and your own Soul.

The Mystical Mirror

So now that we've come this far, Let's focus on the wall behind the Book of Life, as you look at the wall there is a very large black mirror. This black mirror has an unpolished surface and is very deep with no reflection. This mirror is a portal into the unseen regions deep within your mind. As you look into the mirror, this is much like looking into your mind as you are fading off to sleep in a dark room. You can call up certain things, as you ask questions. What does the mirror look like? Is it square, rectangular or round? Let this form for you naturally. Just let the mirror speak to you visually. The black mirror like the Book is alive with energy and very interactive.

For instance as you ask the question to be given information from your Book of Life, you can receive intuitive impressions, written words or passages. Then look up into the black mirror. As you look deep within the mirror you are looking deep within your mind. As you stay present, relaxed and steady you will start to summon images, pictures, imprints or visions coming into view up from the depths. This can be a very vivid experience especially with past lives.

This is the equivalent of what the ancient seers called skrying. To skry for visual details, visions and information the mystics would use a black surface usually obsidian or onyx was preferred because of it's actively psychic qualities, though other materials were also used. This practice is considered to be mystical in nature as is reading the Akashic Records. To be a mystic or to have a mystical experience meant quite simply to look into the myst or into the mysteries.

The fact that we're using the color black does not coincide with any dark practices or symbolism in any way. It's just the best color or complete absence of color to practice bringing or developing images deeply out of the inner mind. Sort of like turning off the lights before bed and watching all the colors, shapes or images in your mind.

So remember the presence of the black mirror in the Great Hall, this will bring you many visions and help to really accelerate your **Akashic Vision**. Remember you are in the Soul energy now during this process so the visuals can be anywhere from dreamy psychic reflections to very detailed and very clear pictures and movies coming from the intuitive Soul body and directly into the Akashic visions.

There is an amazing level of viewing that you can achieve as you are in the Soul energy. You can also practice with any dark or black surface or an actual **skrying mirror** as they are available in some metaphysical or online stores. The real thing that I would have you focus your practice on though is going to be the black unpolished surface of the mirror hanging in the Great Hall of Records. Focus your mind and your energy there and see what images you can allow to come through. They may be nothing short of amazing, but keep your cool. It's best not to go into the Records trying to have an 'over the top' experience. This may or may not yield results. Stay peaceful and balanced as you bring through you clear visions out of the depths of the **Mystical Mirror of the Akasha**.

Let's View Into the Mystical Mirror of the Akashic Records
*Read the Script
and then practice your self guided visualization.*

As you start to relax finding a comfortable place to lay down or sit. Just continue to breathe in and out slowly, deeply and gently. Let go of all of your cares and concerns of the day. As you continue to breathe, visualize your chakras clear and evenly balanced. Visualize a Great Hall peaceful and quiet like a library and stay in this energy of the library. The soft and subtle peace and quiet. As you visualize with your mind, See and travel by thought to the Hall.

As you enter in through the front doors, you look around at the very spacious high ceilings and tall walls. Feel the spaciousness of this room. Notice the very high arched ceiling. The ceiling and the walls are semi-transparent and you can see through them across outer space or through and into different dimensions.

There are stained glass windows lining each side

of the hall. Great beams of colored light are shining down through the windows, as they shine across the floor in colored patterns. As you're standing there you look down at the floor that you now walk across which is so open and spacious. Look at the tiles and look at the detail of the tiles. There are mosaics on the floor tiles that are moving with energy. Look at the patterns of the mosaics. Geometric shapes and patterns, fractals, mandalas. and sacred symbols. Just take a few moments to be in the moment of the Great Hall with it's walls, arched ceilings, tall stained glass windows and mosaic floors.

   As you turn now to look at the altar which holds your great Book of Lifetimes you see on the wall behind the Book a very large mirror. A black mirror which casts no reflection. A responsive portal of your own visions. Take a moment to study the mirror. As you look intently into the black depth. Allow images to come out of the darkness. What do you see? Do you see Messages, Symbols, People, Places or Things? Take your time and enjoy the process… And when you're ready just come back to the Here and Now in this moment.

   Welcome Home.

The Mystical Mirror

Chapter 7
Music of the Spheres

As we continue to move through the Great Hall of the Akashic Records, there are special components which will appear and reappear as we request them to. As we previously talked about dimensional reality and the way that it interacts with our senses and with the flickering patterns of light. Let us now talk about the great spectrum of sound.

From times memorial as far back as we can go, we have within all races of earth culture the earliest styles of making sounds. Some of the earliest versions of humanity and prehistoric man that made sounds such as guttural utterances and tribal calls. These were probably learned by listening to the animals and the sounds of nature. These are some of the earliest versions of call & response communication methods. All of the animals communicated with each other through the flocks, schools and herds by sounds and calls. And by listening to each other. Calls would also have no place or reason without the ability to hear, and most animals have super sensitive hearing. The animals are unique to us in that they do not have (as far as we know) a reasoning mind through which they are able to process past and future.

They do navigate coming moments based on previous learned behaviors through conditioned responses to their environment. This keeps them in the present moment or the Eternal Now Moment. Here in the Now, moments are pure and devoid of trying to project into the past or the future. We could learn a great deal from them about focus in this area.

If we could watch, study and relearn their ability to be free of any other moment except the present moment, our culture might advance peacefully in ways we never even considered. The ability to communicate through sounds, speaking or singing and listening are two very important senses for us as are the rest of our senses.

The ability to uniquely craft a tone from frequency is a magic we often take for granted. As we continue to evolve we continually create newer ways of communicating through sound. We have never lived as a race without sound. It is a very important aspect of nature being aware of itself through interacting, growing and developing.

We laugh, cry, scream, chant, sing, whisper and

talk. And we listen. As we utilize sound itself, we are having an interaction with the frequencies of the **ethers** and through the ethers.

There is a whole spectrum of frequency that we are aware of and some so low or high that they are out of audible range of the human ear. Our frequency spectrum is measured in **Hertz.** The hertz is defined as one cycle per second.

(symbol: Hz) is the derived unit of frequency in the International System of Units (SI) and is defined as one cycle per second. It is named for Heinrich Rudolf Hertz, the first person to provide conclusive proof of the existence of electromagnetic waves. Hertz are commonly expressed in multiples:

kilohertz (10^3 Hz, kHz),
megahertz (10^6 Hz, MHz),
gigahertz (10^9 Hz, GHz),
terahertz (10^{12} Hz, THz),
petahertz (10^{15} Hz, PHz),
exahertz (10^{18} Hz, EHz).

With people, places, interactions, situations and things we often hear each other say: 'I'm getting a good vibe on that' or 'I'm getting a bad vibe'. We are sentiently and energetically sensitive to vibrations of all different kinds:

A certain part of town.
A person who may be acting in a certain way.
A type of music.
A certain interaction between people.

Our own personal situations in life.
and the list goes on...

All things in our world and all things in the Universe are composed of vibrations. Light, sound and colors are all composed of and emitting vibration. Everything can literally be measured in vibration.

Energy medicine or vibrational medicine are used in unique ways as a holistic approach and a unique remedy to some common health themes. Though, if you need a medical doctor's attention best to listen to your gut on that. Never deprive yourself of the attention you need out of fear, denial or neglect.

Music can be colorful and unique in it's vibrational characteristics. Early classical music produced by an orchestra was the first version of surround sound. With the wide range of instruments producing their own tonal responses from low bass through high treble. To watch and to listen to one of the early classical orchestras of Europe must have truly been an amazing experience to behold. The early composers were truly looked at as modern contemporary artists in their day and there were even those who pushed the envelope such as Bach and Beethoven. Hence the term 'Bach and Roll'.

Classical music of all kinds is used in therapy for healing and relaxation, said to have a tonal or vibrational effect on the human body, mind and spirit.

As music evolved through the ages we have many different styles from around the world. Each culture, race or country has at least one style of their own music and in many cases several variations. Early Celtic, Scandinavian, African, Native American, Hindu and Asian are only a few of the many indigenous musics that are available. Each style of music from each culture usually has associated with it a certain apparel, colors, art or dance styles.

In modern times we have many styles of modern as well as traditional music. The modern styles include Country & Western, Rock & Roll, Popular, Rhythm and Blues, and Classical. Many new styles from these have emerged, including New Country, Southern Rock, Heavy Metal, Punk Rock, Disco, Rap, Electronica and many other crossover styles. Many of today's songs are about life, love, sex, hate, fun, family, memories, broken romances, being alone, looking forward, and humor to name a few.

So really we are vibrational beings as one way to look at the human race. We respond to music that reflects our outlook on life. Much in the same way some music has been created (or even contrived) to influence or move humanity in certain response patterns.

Humanity, as a race, in our family life existence and work place have tended to express emotionally in whatever our egos would like to indulge in at the time, be it happy or sad. Some would call this expression of the human spirit. For instance Country music often talks about guys and girls, cowboys and horses, trucks and so forth. Though the origins came from traditional Irish storytelling. Every style has it's own flavor of variable story lines.

Much of our current new music that's created by the younger crowd is a blend of derivatives of other pop culture songs and styles. Music is a creative outlet for all of humanity. Lately we've heard comments from music listeners that the new music doesn't have the same heart and soul that it did several decades ago. Interestingly enough several decades ago people would've said the same thing. Music production had been progressing in a certain direction of quality up to the point that the digital revolution came in.

The spectrum of digitally recorded music lacks the same frequency response and warmth that is available from the older decades of music recorded in analog studios which utilized tape recordings. This is because the frequency response of analog tape recording has a wider range of bandwidth making the sound more dynamic.

In today's music world the vibration of some popular music is low to very low or even dark. Some music is very high in vibration and inspirational. And then there is a whole middle spectrum of music that appeals to most of society.

The Music of the Spheres

Lower vibrations can be attractive for anyone going through difficult times of the emotions or ego. We find that there is an attraction to like minded or heart felt and interpretive messages. The lower vibrations can actually be attractive, magnetic or pull towards someone that is on the edge or close to the same vibrational match. Music can influence our lives. In the same way for someone who is in love and who has just met an attractive person or Soul in their life and is feeling inspired. That person may gravitate towards higher vibrational love songs of the heart that were inspired by the writer about meeting the love of their life. So it all comes back to frequency and vibration.

In many sacred texts, writings and teachings, we've heard about a unique wonderful music coming from the higher dimensions. The **Music of the Spheres**. This music is said to be emanating the frequencies and tones that generate the constructs of the Universe and reality itself. Divine tones of the higher realms with a tonal spectrum that permeates everything and rings out across all time and space. As these frequencies ring out they dance, intermingle, influence and interact with all other known spectral frequencies to some degree.

The spherical music's origin of broadcast is a grand set of spheres that are located within the Great Hall of Records. In the higher dimensional realms they can literally be summoned to different locations by thought or can be travelled to by teleportation to the location of the Spheres by acknowledgement through focus of thought or vibrational connection such as love. To realize the existence of the Spheres can be done through learning about them in studies such as this, or you may find them on your own either floating in the higher dimensions or within the Great Hall of Records.

The Great Spheres are clear transparent and crystalline in appearance. One sphere suspended within another, within another, within another and so on. The spheres are floating perfectly suspended within each other floating as if by magic. The super high, fine and clear vibration is what keeps the perfect light transparent spheres in flotation one within the next.

The Great Spheres are like other elements of the Great Hall. They can morph into plain sight when needed. They may seem to be hidden to us when we enter into the Records. Much like the Records are hidden to us here in this reality. As we need to travel to the Records they become visible, whether it's by a guided journey process or by more of an instantaneous shift into the Records that we may have attained by practice. The same is true with the great Spheres and their tonal frequency broadcast.

So as the Spheres are broadcasting a wide spectrum of Divine sounds, we can connect with them and be brought right up into the higher dimensions to them floating in the space of the higher dimensions. As they can be in many places at once, they broadcast their presence out in multiple directions when and where needed at different intensities.

The spheres represent the worlds within worlds of all dimensions coexisting within one another. The coexistence of worlds or dimensions actually occupy the same space and time though time and space may occur more relative in nature. And then there are other worlds that occupy other spaces and versions of time in remote regions.

The geometrical representation of the Spheres is symbolically the closest way that they can be illustrated in this heavenly inter-dimensional dynamic. This is also a grand depiction of the Angelic Realm. The Angelic Realm is spherical in nature and operates with energy emanations coming from within and projecting out. Great spheres of the Angelic Realms occupy space around our planet.

The Music of the Spheres is projecting out from within. The frequencies being perpetual, they are literally the singing rebroadcast of the starlight cosmic frequencies. And even higher, finer purer projections. Beaming out in all directions simultaneously through all dimensions and through all space and time. Think about that for a moment. Is it possible that this 'music of the spheres' frequencies is reaching us and we're not aware of it? Remember the constructs of the Universe itself are all made from different layers and levels of vibration. So the Great Spheres are much like a radio broadcast tower. Just a more highly evolved and pure light manifestation of Divine Intelligence.

The Music of these Spheres has the power to clear one's energy fields. Just standing in the presence of the Spheres within the Great Hall can be transformational. They can also shift your vibration. Clearing a person's frequencies and then shifting or lifting your personal energy to a clearer and lighter variation of tonal responses. As you may well know, this can have an immediate effect on a person's outlook, their emotional state, their mental health and freedom, and even physical healing can occur. So resetting the tones and frequencies within your body, mind and spirit with the Great Spheres can bring about great change.

What is their job and purpose, these Great Spheres? To sing the full Universal tonal spectrums of All Truth, All Love, All Light, All Creation in the true fashion of the Akashic Records. This is the realm of the Ascended Masters. The Higher Worlds. As Jesus Christ was once quoted as saying "My fathers house has many mansions." Worlds upon worlds, or should we say worlds within worlds?

In Atlantis there was a great set of these Spheres as the Music of the Light rang out across the planet. And as Atlantis fell, the great time shift occurred as the photon field that the Earth, our solar system and the galaxy passed through became intensely active with light energy. The Earth's magnetic poles were greatly shifted out of it's normal alignment, and the magnetic field of the planet was wiped out. As this happened erratic weather patterns wreaked havoc across this world. Many lives were lost both human and animal. In a state of planetary emergency there came alien races by ship that were already aware of the turmoil being caused on a galactic level. They worked to restore the electromagnetic fields of our planet and the rest of the solar system.

As the great shift occurred. The mind fields of humans here were interrupted by being unable to speak or think. As our neighbors from off world came down and rebalanced those who were put into leadership roles as 'priests' of the societies in that age, they were restored mentally and energetically as the 'visitors' started to restore the natural energetic grid of planet Earth. As they brought the energy grid back online by installing pyramids and great spheres that were singing with frequency deep down in the hidden halls of the Earth.

As in the ancient stories which refer to the Halls of Amenti, Great pyramids were erected around the earth that helped to balance the 4th dimensional spectrum which also helped to organize or house the mental spectrum of man and animals here in the 3rd dimension. This must have had an effect on the 5th dimensional astral world, the 6th dimensional Angelic Realm and on up into other dimensions with the same or varied intensities across all dimensions. Let us look into the Great Hall for the rest of the story as we Journey into the Akashic Records and look into the Ancient History of our world and beyond as we connect with the Music of the Spheres.

Let's View Into the Music of the Spheres in the Akashic Records
Read the Script
and then practice your self guided visualization.

As you start to relax finding a comfortable place to lay down or sit. Just continue to breathe in and out slowly, deeply and gently. Let go of all of your cares and concerns of the day. As you continue to breathe, visualize your chakras clear and evenly balanced. Visualize a Great Hall peaceful and quiet like a library and stay in this energy of the library. The soft and subtle peace and quiet. As you visualize with your mind, See and travel by thought to the Hall. As you enter in through the front doors, you look around at the very spacious high ceilings and tall walls.

Feel the spaciousness of this room. Notice the very high arched ceiling. The ceiling and the walls are semi-transparent and you can see through them across outer space or through and into different dimensions.

There are stained glass windows lining each side of the hall. Great beams of colored light are shining down through the windows, as they shine across the floor in colored patterns. As you're standing there you look down at the floor that you now walk across which is so open and spacious.

Look at the tiles and look at the detail of the tiles. There are mosaics on the floor tiles that are moving with energy. Look at the patterns of the mosaics. Geometric shapes and patterns, fractals, mandalas and sacred symbols. Just take a few moments to be in the moment of the Great Hall with it's walls, arched ceilings, tall stained glass windows and mosaic floors.

As you turn now to look at the altar which holds your Great Book of Lifetimes you see on the wall behind the Book, a very large mirror which casts no reflection. A responsive portal of your own visions.

And now turn and look in the center of the room you see appearing before you a very large set of crystaline glass spheres. One floating inside the next, inside the next, inside the next. The Spheres are singing with tones that emanate waves of sound, light and color. Take a few moments to listen and watch and as you observe the spheres notice what they have to show you or their influence. Listen to the singing tones and how they vibrate your whole being. They move through you healing you and clearing you. The divine tones accompanied by colors that ring and vibrate through creation.

Take a few moments to connect in and study the Spheres and their music...And when you're ready just come back to the Here and Now in this moment. Welcome Home.

The Music of the Spheres

Chapter 8
Rooms & Sections of the Records

The Akashic Records in it's entirety would take lifetimes to traverse through the vast amount of information that is held within these etheric walls. Created for the purpose of a storehouse of all knowledge where the Souls come to gather wisdom, experience healing and learning in between lifetimes. Could this literally be part of heaven? Yes. The Grace that emanates from this place is immense. The Healing vibrations of peace that sing through the halls. As a storehouse for the Books of Life for all Souls who have ever visited the Earth, are here now incarnate and those just coming in, the connections to all these Souls are here in this place. As the Souls radiate their energy this must be a place of great vibrations of Divine frequency. As you study energy on your path and the different forms of healing and energy work you have come into contact with and even some great healers who have demonstrated powerful energy, you have felt the projections of energy from different techniques and from other healers or psychics. So your body, your senses, your mind and nervous system are all capable of having an experience with the sensations of projected energy.

When we have these types of energy experiences it can give us a 'wow' factor feeling. And often because of that we want to feel more. This is natural for people to want to have a tangible experience with energy. The more energy involved the more tangible the experience.

Sometimes the source of projected energy might not be as clean or pure as a person might prefer. People are often eager to start having sensations with energy when they start their studies and that can lead to coming in contact with varied levels of energy. This is a component of why there are so many variable levels of truth, healing and the light that are filtered through different individuals, modalities of energy work, and/or spiritual organizations.

All of that said, the energy of your Soul or another person's Soul is quite often hard to sense or feel. Every spiritual path and it's teachings and writings talk about the Soul in relation to people, followers, practitioners, etc. But not how to feel or experience the Soul. This is what these Akashic Records studies are all about. Having a sentient experience with your

Soul energy. Coming into contact and getting to know the higher levels of your own true being. Once you tap into yourself on this level, you are changed. You now have access to your core self, your Higher Self like never before.

This will bring you into contact with truer and higher levels of more pure and clear energy. Once you get to this level it will be more easy for you to discern lower or less clear forms and levels of energy. So from this place and the knowing of the true power and radiance of your own Soul, imagine the multiplied, amplified energies of all the radiant Soul energies that must be waiting for you to experience within the Records! Not that you will be tapping into others' Soul energy, but you will certainly feel the presence of it by osmosis and *that* in and of itself is nothing short of amazing.

As you are also in your Soul energy and connecting into the Akashic Records and visiting this grand place, the other Soul presences their will help you to feel your own Soul's energy as all Souls are part of Creator God of Love. Are you starting to get a sense of the importance of this? So you are not just going to the Akashic Records for an energy experience. As we experience so many different kinds of energy work, it's easy sometimes to become 'energy junkies' or to continually want to partake of more and more energy. Make sure this is not your reasoning for connecting with the Records or your information is likely to be skewed.

Again, this is Heaven we're talking about, or part of it, and there's no limitation as to what we can experience there in our Akashic Journeys. The only limitation is any conflicts within the self (your self). This is why from my perspective we should always have a sense of reverence present when visiting this place.

As you visit the Great Hall you are sure to meet the Keeper of the Records from time to time. This very tall and kindly being of white light will help guide you to your Book of Lifetimes or to a certain section that you may want or need to visit to get healing or information from. The Keeper may show up in various ways. I personally have experienced three different versions of them (more on this in Vol. 3). The Keeper of the Records, the Arc Angels, or the Ascended Masters may meet you there from time to time to give you life guidance whether in guided meditations, dreams or waking state thoughts.

As you visit the Records you are most usually guided to your personal Book of Lifetimes which reveals information past, present and future about your Life's Path and your Soul's Journey. For some of us we may see books and for others scrolls laid out on tables. Some people go in and immediately start to see great shelves full of books lining the main hall.

Next there is your interaction with the books. Are you moving towards shelves or another room to get the books? Are the books or scrolls coming to you in some way? Is someone bringing you the books? These are all creative variations of your visual connections with the higher dimensions.

As you become well versed with accessing the Records continually and getting information for yourself or others, you find more ease and grace in doing so. Have you ever wondered if there is more? Have you ever wondered why or where there could be more information concerning the history of the world and other subjects?

I have found great sections and even entire rooms which are filled with different classifications of subjects concerning the world we live in and the world we live on. As I was guided by my Higher Self through dreams and also through intentional inquiries in guided meditations, I found great store houses of information with vault-like rooms. These rooms would appear inter-dimensionally and reveal themselves as needed like a catalogue system.

As I would intend myself in a certain direction energetically with a question in mind, a doorway would appear revealing a room full of relics pertaining to world history or ancient cultures. A room containing the history of our planet, the solar system and it's place within our galaxy. A room dedicated to all of the cultures and races of the world. Another special room dedicated to inventions and so on.

There is a special room also dedicated to the arts and

art forms. In the center of this room is a holographic pedestal which streams ideas, art forms, creations and inventions. It is very interesting and amazing to watch. There is a room dedicated completely to healing of the physical body, energy bodies, mind and spirit. So if you are involved in medical intuitive work, this will be an area of great importance. There is a room pertaining to light beings and angels and the Good. There is also a room that catalogues dark spirits, beings and entities. This can come in really handy, if you're doing shamanic work or clearing.

There is also room where you will find all of the great personalities, philosophers, artists, inventors, politicians, humanitarians and even celebrities. This is very unique to stand in their presence and even more so to have conversations with them. These rooms are like a second level of the work. Once you've mastered going into your own Book of Life for your own healing and self awakening process, the next level of work will be accessing greater levels of knowledge for the rest of your life. This is the great work, to truly know yourself and to know the rest of the world, others, and the Universe through that lens. Once you start to see the immensity of what's available, it really becomes quite humbling for any one of us to come into contact with all of this.

Rooms & Sections of the Records

Let's View the Rooms and Sections of the Akashic Records
*Read the Script
and then practice your self guided visualization.*

As you start to relax finding a comfortable place to lay down or sit. Just continue to breathe in and out slowly, deeply and gently. Let go of all of your cares and concerns of the day. As you continue to breathe, visualize your chakras clear and evenly balanced. Visualize a Great Hall peaceful and quiet like a library and stay in this energy of the library. The soft and subtle peace and quiet. As you visualize with your mind, See and travel by thought to the Hall. As you enter in through the front doors, you look around at the very spacious high ceilings and tall walls. Feel the spaciousness of this room. Notice the very high arched ceiling. The ceiling and the walls are semi-transparent and you can see through them across outer space or through and into different dimensions.

There are stained glass windows lining each side of the hall. Great beams of colored light are shining down through the windows, as they shine across the floor in colored patterns. As you're standing there you look down at the floor that you now walk across. So open and spacious. Look at the tiles and look at the detail of the tiles.

There are mosaics on the floor tiles that are moving with energy. Look at the patterns of the mosaics. Geometric shapes and patterns, fractals, mandalas and sacred symbols. Just take a few moments to be in the presence of the Great Hall with it's walls, arched ceilings, tall stained glass windows and mosaic floors.

Now as you look around the room, look for doorways and hallways to other adjoining rooms. These other rooms are specialty rooms of study. Just acknowledge and view their entrance. Do you see now any new or different features to the room which you're now in? Do you see tables for study, shelves for archiving, books or ancient scrolls? What else do you see? Take a moment to study. And when you're ready just come back to the Here and Now in this moment.

Welcome Home.

Rooms & Sections of the Records

Chapter 9

THE UPPER CHAMBER OF THE AKASHA

*A*s we continue delving into the many aspects of the Great Hall of Records, much like the dynamic of filling in the characters from our gallery of past lives. We are building a creative and visionary case. We see into the Great Hall with our creative minds and as we do so we interact mentally, energetically and on a locally quantified streaming focus of energy. Our vision is interacting with the Great Hall through our Soul energy as we connect into the feeling of peace and solitude of the place.

As we spoke of in previous chapters, the walls and ceilings are translucent or transparent. This is partially due to the inter-dimensional nature of the place itself and where it is located. There is a super high speed flickering of light in time-space reality here on Planet Earth and throughout the Universe. The light of the cosmos reaches us here in the denser atmosphere or 3D reality and it causes everything to flicker with energy. Like a movie or a 'motion picture' this is a very unique component of our reality.

This is part of the backdrop of our animate movie of life. As you consider this dynamic it will be a good thing to think about and take into your mind as you're visualizing, creating and manifesting your life's path. The stars glisten in the night sky and flicker with this same energy. The Cosmic Energy of Creation. Everywhere present in the Universe is this cosmic flickering effect or vibration.

As we refer to the walls and ceiling of the Great Akashic Hall being semi-transparent to fully transparent, this is due to the flickering energy as well. The energy flickers at different rates and speeds throughout the higher dimensions. We tend to refer to the other dimensions as being higher. They are really more like parallel dimensions though we number them in sequence and tend to stack them one upon the other to get our minds around the idea of more than our current reality.

The dimensions vibrate at higher, clearer or finer varying rates of speed. They are all interwoven and all relatively occupying the same space at the same time. We do have separations or pockets where the energy of the dimensions vortex together and are clearer or thinner. A certain ebb and flow if you will, full of currents, fields, eddies, streams, rivers and oceans of dimensional time-space flickering realities. Ever beginning and never ending. This also includes the Great Hall of Records.

Though, the Great Hall has an even more subtle location and vibration. As it truly operates from the 'in between' of space time dimensions. This is what gives it that extra ever so peaceful feel along with extra natural levels of protection. So as you continue to practice your access with the Records you will continue to become more accustomed to familiarizing yourself with the different dimensions. You will at least know the difference between lower denser energy and higher, lighter, finer energy.

As the energy flickers throughout the dimensions there becomes another created dynamic we may have not previously considered. Different variations of the Records for people at different levels of practice. Another self protect element of the Akashic Records system. So if someone were to start accessing the Records whether by accident or intention and they aren't really in a place within themselves to take in the clarity and knowledge that accessing with their true Book of Life might bring to them. They may be guided to an astral version or a 5th dimensional version of the Temple. This is where the dynamics, elements and energies are simplified or stepped down. If someone is going through a rough patch or dark time in their life, they may only be able to handle certain levels of information and vibration.

So now at different levels of vibration whether simplified for the astral plane or enhanced for the advanced levels of the Records, there are other locations and some are connections through the ethers to interesting places within the earth plane.

One similar dynamic you may want to look at is that of the great cathedrals and castles of the world. Their amazing structures and uniquely ornamental decor. Their symmetrical and sacred geometrical designs. Is it any wonder that we have accessed creatively by way of ancient and mystical groups, a grand temple to visit in the higher ethers? Was the grand temple in the higher ethers of the dimensions already there? Did humanity need more mystical practice to process the ideas of how the energy is stepping down in vibration as much as it sometimes evolves into the higher dimensions?

As we now know of the flickering animation of energy; disappearing and reappearing from within the time space dimensions. And as we see now that the energy of the walls and the ceilings within the Great Hall are viewable and translucent as they allow for what's beyond the structure to be brought into an intimate distance of perspective that you may not readily measure through depth. Things may appear near and far at the same time. In the same

The Upper Chamber

way there are available the other rooms and sections which are vibrating at super high rates of thought from the Universal God Mind.

As we need them, or call them to us, these sections become revealed to us. You may access the Records over a period of time and never have an experience with the other rooms and sections and then one day there is a need for it when you're dealing with a certain situation and are then granted instant access. Allowing for this dynamic of the Hall and time-space actually giving way and revealing a deeper and more expansive levels and sections of the Records.

So in the same way we now bring your attention to what we will refer to as the **Upper Chamber** of the Great Hall of the Akashic Records. There is actually an upper level to this great temple that operates in the same way. It is in the even higher finer flickering time space realities. And when you want to ask for passage to the upper chamber it is granted. There are many unique qualities about the nature of the upper chamber.

As we tend ourselves up through the ceiling through a stained glass skylight that is marked with sacred geometries, we may feel a gentle pressure on our crown or a buzzing of energy around the top of our heads as we move up into the Higher Chamber of the Records.

This is truly a unique place and also operates like a portal of energy. So as you are moving up through the energy and you arrive you can see that there are different things around the room. I usually see multiple books or scrolls laid out for examination. These wisdom writings and higher vibrational light language messages of the Akasha are all here for your reading. That is for the adept that has taken the time to practice and sees the virtue of the work.

This is the area of quietude where you may really get into looking at the Akashic symbols and spending time with their interpretation. The more time you take to look at the light symbol language and to bring that vibration into your eyes and your mind, the more you will be able to read and to transform the passages into other forms of communicative language for earth plane studying. Translation of these **Akashic Light Symbols** into earth language, symbols and drawings. When you get to this stage you will have known your life perspectives on many levels to change.

As you look around you are in the room which is square or rectangular for the most part, though there is another shape shifting quality to it. As there is a golden **Flower of Life** on the floor that is moving, turning, and vibrating with patterns of energy, life giving energies of creation. The walls also may seem to be round or octagonal. As the books and scrolls are still laid out on tables around the room. What else do you see? There could also be tools for drawing and reading, spectacles and magnifying glasses. A compass, ruler or drawing utensils.

Sometimes we may experience the round or octagonal walls as a steeple in the ceiling of the room that you may float up to and look out of. This is where you can see the Light of the Sun coming to you so close. And you can witness the light symbols of the Akasha coming from the sun in through the window to greet you, as now they continue to stream in. The sun has it's own set of master Akashic Records that are used for the Sun or 'Sol' itself, as do all of the planets. Mercury, Venus, Urantia(Earth), Mars, Saturn, Jupiter, Neptune, Uranus and Pluto. Though the light symbols reaching us here are intended for the Earth.

As you look up into the Light you are going to notice that in this dome or steeple there are 8 suns or eight worlds as you turn about. As you look through each window you tune into a different time and place, a different dimension, a different Now. You may also experience Omnipresence in your vision which is more of a 360 degree view. This opens your mind's eye and your consciousness in new and unique ways. All of these elements of the Upper Chamber are alive with energy and giving to You as they shift You into new levels of reading the Records and of time space reality itself.

LET'S VIEW INTO THE UPPER CHAMBER OF THE AKASHIC RECORDS
*Read the Script
and then practice your self guided visualization.*

As you start to relax finding a comfortable place to lay down or sit. Just continue to breathe in and out slowly, deeply and gently. Let go of all of your cares and concerns of the day. As you continue to breathe, visualize your chakras clear and evenly balanced.

Visualize a Great Hall peaceful and quiet like a library and stay in this energy of the library. The soft and subtle peace and quiet. As you visualize with your mind, See and travel by thought to the Hall. As you enter in through the front doors, you look around at the very spacious high ceilings and tall walls. Feel the spaciousness of this room. Notice the very high arched ceiling. The ceiling and the walls are semi-transparent and you can see through them across outer space or through and into different dimensions.

There are stained glass windows lining each side of the Hall. Great beams of colored light are shining down through the windows, as they shine across the floor in colored patterns. As you're standing there you look down at the floor that you now walk across. So open and spacious. Look at the tiles and look at the detail of the tiles. There are mosaics on the floor tiles that are moving with energy. Look at

THE UPPER CHAMBER

the patterns of the mosaics. Geometric shapes and patterns, fractals, mandalas and sacred symbols. Just take a few moments to be in the moment of the Great Hall with it's walls, arched ceilings, tall stained glass windows and mosaic floors.

Now as you look around the room, look for doorways and hallways to other adjoining rooms. These other rooms are specialty rooms of study. Just acknowledge and view their entrance. Do you see now any new or different features to the room which you're now in? Do you see tables for study, shelves for archiving, ancient scrolls? What else do you see?

As you turn now to look at the altar which holds your great Book of Lifetimes you see on the wall behind the book a very large mirror. A black mirror which casts no reflection. A responsive portal of your own visions.

As you now move over to a stairway that leads up to a hallway where there is a door. As you enter in through the door you see a great chamber filled with artifacts and power objects. Akashic symbols and language. Scrolls and books laid out to read. Windows that let you view out over 8 directions. Take a moment to study this chamber and the expanded gifts it has to offer. Just familiarize yourself with this room and take your time... And when you're ready just come back to the Here and Now in this moment. Welcome Home.

Exercise 1

Exploring within the Akashic Hall of Records

*Read the Script
and then practice your self guided visualization.*

*A*s you start to relax finding a comfortable place to lay down or sit. Just continue to breathe in and out slowly, deeply and gently. Let go of all of your cares and concerns of the day. As you continue to breathe, visualize your chakras clear and evenly balanced. As your chakras are clear and evenly balanced, look now at the colors of your chakras. The Base chakra at your tailbone is a deep ruby red. The Sacral chakra along your spine adjacent from your naval is a beautiful bright orange. Your Solar plexus is a bright, golden yellow. Your Heart center along the spine is shining a very bright emerald green. As your throat center is emanating a super cool blue. Your 3rd eye is glowing with a very deep rich royal blue or indigo energy. And your crown is shining with a beautiful deep violet. See all of these colors along your spine shining very brightly. As they shine brightly they are clear, healthy and balanced and your kundalini energy is moving up your spine continuously. The energy is flowing up your spine continuously in a balanced manner.

See now and visualize a beautiful bright shaft of light, a portal forming around you that gently grows brighter and brighter. As the column of energy continues to grow bright everything else in the room continues to fade back or grow dimmer or darker. As you're relaxing and sitting in this great pillar of white light. The white light is now permeating your skin, your body, mind and spirit. Clearing you and lifting you up, up and away. Up, up and away as you feel yourself becoming lighter and lighter you start to float up through the portal of light.

As you float up through the heavens you move through the upper atmosphere. Becoming lighter you are leaving your room through the ceiling and continue to glide up. You recognize the distant glow of the stars and celestial bodies as you continue to travel up. Continuing up you soon come into a great bank of white clouds. The pure white glow takes your sight away, but that's okay, your Soul knows the way.

Exploring within the Records

    As you feel a gentle sensation at the crown of your head, you come up through the clouds and find yourself standing before a very large temple building atop the clouds. Notice the features from the outside. Just take your time to look at the features of the exterior. As you view the front entrance there are 4 pronounced steps that lead up to the front doors. A very large set of wooden doors. Just take a moment to look at these very large wooden doors. See the tone of the wood. Are there any carvings? What is the design? As you proceed to walk up the steps now....1....2....3....4....you now face the front doors here on the landing.

    There are two statues, one of a lion on the right side of the door and one of a lioness on the left side of the door. As you step onto the landing they both come to life and are very real. As you stand before them, they let you know with their eyes that they are the grand protectors here of this place. While you are inside they will be on watchful guard. Reach down now and stroke the main of the lion. As your eyes connect you can feel the lions' loving gaze.

    As the doors open to you naturally and silently as if by the thought intention alone to enter, exposing the interior of the very large and grand hall.

    Stepping inside you see many interesting and colorful features. There are very tall and large stained glass windows. These stained glass windows are backlit by the cosmic star energy that flows in through them. Just take a few moments to view now these Windows to the Cosmos, the beautiful stained glass windows. As the star energy flows down in beams across the Hall it lights the amazing mosaics that are lining all the tiles of the great floor. The cosmic starlight seems to be animating these mosaic patterns. Take a moment to view and observe these patterns. The movements of the designs can be subtle or very pronounced. Their energy can flow with your energy as you walk across them or stand still and as your energy ebbs and flows.

Pan now your vision around the room. As you turn very slowly in a clockwise circle looking at everything there is to see in the Great Hall and feeling the wide open space. As you pan around notice now over the doors where you entered there is a very large and colorful tapestry. This tapestry is shining with luminescent and pearlescent colors.

There are waves of colors moving through the tapestry. This is the Tapestry of Souls. A moving picture of all the Souls who have visited the earth plane and are here now whether in physical form or between lives. The waves of moving color represent changes or expressions moving through the group consciousness of the **Collective Soul of Humanity**, whether it be mental, spiritual, physical or emotional. These energetic shifts show changes expressing through varied levels of love, enlightenment, emotional, mental and spiritual learning. Just take a few moments to observe the Tapestry of Souls and the patterns running through it.

As you continue to pan around the room now coming back to front and center and looking down the length of the Hall to the other end, the north end. Notice now that there is a very large and old wooden table. More of an altar. Look at the detail of this altar like table. Are there carvings? What is the color and grain of the wood? Just take a moment to study it.

As you walk closer now to the ancient table you see now that there is a very ancient book, a very large book laid out and open to the middle page. This is your Book of Life *or* Book of Lifetimes. As you move closer to it you notice that it has a certain living, breathing quality. It is made of the same energy as your Soul Essence. As you feel and view this energy connection that is yours, notice the quality and features of the Book. You may take a few moments now to view into and connect with the Book.

There is one very large white candle on the table behind the book. This candle shines a peaceful still eternal flame. It is burning here symbolizing and as the Eternal Now Moment forever endlessly through time. Just take a few moments to visualize and study or focus on this Holy Flame and experience the Eternal Now continuum.

On the wall behind the Altar and your Book there hangs a very large and black mirror. The surface is unpolished and casts no reflection. The mirror is actually also a window into eternity, of which you can call images out of the pitch black tone. This allows your mind to form images out of the window. As the Mystical Mirror is part of the Akashic Hall of Wisdom it is charged with the energy of the stars and the cosmos for creative viewing. Just take a few moments to study this large black mystical mirror and it's unique qualities.

As you now turn around to the center of the room, there now appears a grand set of crystalline Spheres. As they sit on a metallic base composed purely of elements of our world. The very large outside sphere has another inside it perfectly and proportionately suspended within. Within that sphere another, and within that one another and so on and so forth. 144 spheres as they appear to move down in size infinitely, perfectly energetically suspended each one within the next. The Great Spheres are singing with the Music of the Spheres. The tones, frequencies and songs that are present in all dimensions and vibrate with the tones of all things. Holding the **Divine Composition** of All things. They also help to heal, clear and shift a person's Soul, Light Body and Total Self. Just take a moment to listen to the songs, tones and frequencies of the Music of the Spheres and to be in the presence of the Spheres.

As you move freely about the Hall now looking around, you start to notice that as you move towards a wall it instantly opens previously invisible doorways and hallways into other rooms. These connecting rooms have specific collections of knowledge and information. Just take a few moments to browse the connecting rooms and the different energetic feel of each of the certain rooms and their collections, whether few or many, just take few moments here.

Now as you look up towards the very high arch ceilings you sense there is another floor or another story to the Great Hall. How you get there is creatively up to you. You may use a special spiral staircase or a stairway. You may also float up into the room through an energetic portal or opening, or simply intend your self to appear into the room, into this Upper Chamber. As you appear into the upper chamber take a view around the room of all the energy tools for creating and reading the scrolls and Records. Notice that there are eight windows. One for each direction on each of the 8 walls creating an oblong octagon shaped room. On the floor and the ceiling there is a 12 pointed star. This room holds the higher knowledge and directions to other Akashic Records systems in other star systems and on other planets. Just take a few moments to view this Upper Chamber of the Records and familiarize yourself with it.

Now that you've become a bit more experienced with your Akashic Energy Vision to creatively explore all of the main aspects of the Akashic Hall of Records, just come back to the main room and offer a few words of gratitude for the opportunity to be in the presence of this sacred place.

As you move back across the Hall to the front doors noticing some of the features in the room as you exit. Stepping out onto the front landing the lions greet you. They have been waiting to say hello and goodbye to you. As they once again become inanimate stone statues, you continue down the 4 steps. 4....3....2....1.... as you step across the clouds the portal or column of white and golden energy appears once again. As you're suspended within it, you start to float down through the clouds once again. Moving through the cosmos, seeing all of the beautiful celestial bodies, you now see planet Earth coming closer.

See the bright blue of the oceans and the white glow of the atmosphere against the backdrop of space. Coming closer now to your part of the world and now to your area. Coming back down into your home and now into your physical body. Wiggle your fingers and toes to bring yourself more fully into the body. Blink your eyes and take a deep breath.

Welcome Home. We Thank Creator God, The Universal Energies and the Keepers of the Records for a grand experience of the Great Akashic Hall of Wisdom. Om Peace Amen.

Exercise 2
OM Meditation with the Sri Yantram

*A*ll things in the universe are truly vibrating with sound and light from within the known and hidden frequency spectrums. As we look around at the known physical world and our surroundings, we witness the pure truth of the world as it is. Appearing before our eyes in one continual expression of intertwined moments, instances, events, people, places and things, through, light, color, sound, action and awareness both known and unknown.

The dreamer's dream of reality and life lived through all of it's known expressions that we see around us. How is it possible? That we have lived a mundane physical life existence and also have within us the potential to see more than one perspective of reality? The immensity and simplicity of it all is enough to bring us into what I like to call moments

of enlightenment. When we become aware that there is more than this moment and that this moment Is All there is. In the same place, time and space all one.

The ancient yogis of India and the energy masters of the far east, would use their voices to create tones. And as they experimented with the tones, they developed the ancient language of Sanskrit.

Sanskrit is comprised of syllables that create specific vibrations. These vibrations are used to vibrate certain parts of the body for purposes of healing, manifesting, clearing or enlightenment.

The syllables of Sanskrit are used in prayers and

chants called mantras. Mantras are used repeatedly or in certain times and places for certain parts of the body or certain rituals such as holidays, birthdays, weddings, funerals, and communing with God, etc. They are also used for clearing, healing and manifesting.

I thoroughly recommend studying the usage of chanted, spoken and silent mantras. The most common and the mother of all mantras is Om.

Om represents the vibration of all things continuously. Om represents also the oneness and inter-connectedness of all things in a femininely charged way. As the ancient yogis traveled to the other side of the veil past our known reality, they heard a tone. A continual vibrating or humming sound. As they came back from their journeys they put this tone into the vocal sound expression of 'Om'.

Try this sound, if you haven't been exposed to it already. Simply take a deep breath in and chant in the tone that's most comfortable for you.....

The sound OM (with a long O)

OOOOOOOOOOOOOOMMMMMMMMMMM
OOOOOOOOOOOOOOMMMMMMMMMMM
OOOOOOOOOOOOOOMMMMMMMMMMM

Feel the vibration from it within your body. See how it makes you feel. At first you may naturally feel the oneness effect from chanting this sound. If you're feeling stressed and need a quick reset without the thought process of more advanced techniques, this will be very effective for you.

The Om is both simple and effective. The more you work with the mantra and sound the more it will work with you. The sound Om is like an ocean of vibration literally permeating all things. You may think of it as all things in the Universe are composed of this base vibration and singing with the tone Om. As you continue to use the sound. You may use it as a low tone that vibrates your body more deeply or as a mid to high pitched tone that will vibrate your head.

As you chant the Om sound pay attention to feeling it in your body. Feel your whole body or different parts of your body vibrating with the sound. Now also try a mid to higher pitched tone and listen to the frequency. Open up your nasal and head passages with your throat and let it vibrate your whole head. This will give you an amazing sensation. You may feel energy in and around your head buzzing and vibrating as you do this.

Now let's talk about the Sri Yantram. Please see the illustration in this section. This is an ancient Mandala which is a pictorial representation of the energy flow of the sound Om. This yantram depicts the masculine and the feminine energies. The masculine energies are depicted by the upright pyramids going from smaller to larger in a sequence symbolizing vibration which is emanating from

Source. The feminine energy of the Universe and/or realities is symbolized by the inverted or upside down pyramids one within the next also emanating out from Source as the receptive chalice. As you will notice the upright and the inverted pyramids are intertwined together symbolizing the All or the Oneness of the Universe. The Uni-verse, one verse, one song.

As you now look at the picture of the Sri Yantram. This is an ancient tantric practice. You can view into this picture or find another that may suit your viewing fancy. Maybe you already have a Sri Yantram.

As you look into the center of the Sri Yantram chant the sound Om. This is the ancient practice. Using the sound while looking at a picture that represents the sound.

Now as you're looking at the diagram and you're chanting the sound Om, next, look at the pyramid and inverted pyramid sequences and think of the left and right hemispheres of your brain.

The feminine or inverted pyramid sequences represent the right side of the brain, which is responsible for communicating with the left side or feminine side of the body and expresses through creativity.

The masculine or upright pyramid sequences represent the left side of the brain, which is responsible for communicating with the right side or masculine side of the body and expresses through logic.

Once you have the idea of these dynamics incorporated easily through thought during your meditation, next visualize the elements of earth, fire, water, air and bring them to your mind field and your brain as you attract them and radiate them simultaneously.

The capstone of this process is that now in the oneness of this Om, continue and add that which you would simply like to attract or manifest. It will be easier and more powerful if you focus on one thing at a time.

The key is to read through this try not to make it complicated. It is a detailed description, though as you move through it in your mind, let the process speak to you and unfold for you naturally. The focus of expansion is that you are attempting to experience a few things simultaneously. So move from one part to the next and visualize that they are all working at the same time as you bring in each element of this meditation process.

Now you have experienced the ancient oneness of the Sri Yantram Om meditation, activated the left and right sides of your brain, and practiced at harnessing the elements as you visualize a single pointed vision for manifesting. This is a process that you can use in varying stages as you open your mind and continue to ready yourself for higher and deeper levels of Journeys into the Akashic Records.

Om Shri Yantram Meditation

Chapter 10
Ancestral Healing with the Records

When we first find the Akashic Records or we are guided to it, there are usually reasons for it either known or unknown at the time. One of the reasons we may be guided to the Records could be ancestral healing and clearing.

Throughout our lives and on our journey home we sometimes have a quest to know more or to find out why things are working the way they have been in our lives. Often times there can be silent invisible road blocks which keep us from living our true potential. One of the processes that some people experience could be an on-going sadness or feeling of failure. Maybe a person feels inferior to others, life or their surroundings. Some people even feel such uneasiness in their life that they may develop physical problems as a way of trying to compensate for their self imposed short comings.

There are a whole myriad of different creative, energetic and physical excuses that some of us experience as a way of balancing the things in our lives and within ourselves that we cannot seem to come to grips with or to make peace with. Well noted here, when this does occur, start your self healing right away. Don't wait until the denial turns into symptoms which may point to other possible risks. If you need help in your process reach out to a healer for help and get yourself back in the zone or into a better place within yourself possibly much better than you were before. Work smart and balanced.

The mind, body, energy systems, the emotions, the astral body, the nervous, digestive and cardiovascular systems....All these integral parts and systems of our Total Self seek expression and balance in relation to our lives and things we've experienced. Whether it be social integrational skills, community interaction, learning earlier in life or recovering from an illness whether minor or life challenging. The body, mind and spirit always seek recovery no matter what the challenge is. Another dynamic that can occur is that sometimes we might feel fear and we feel lost to illnesses or situations.

The great yogi Paramahansa Yogananda once stated: "We all seek to do our very best at everything we participate in no matter what it may be." We tend to want to do our very best at everything whether it's good, bad or indifferent for us. This is also an expression of the Universal energy creatively moving through us. So as drama comes up for us in the body, mind, emotions or spirit, we often feel it and participate very colorfully. Another dynamic that occurs is that through a tendency for survival of the psyche, mind, body and emotions can tend to shove or stuff things down for processing at some later time.

Sometimes there can be denial associated with situations surrounding life events. If there is severe enough trauma, the body, mind, emotions and psyche will block it out from a person's memory so they can continue to live a somewhat functional life. There may be colorations in a person's psychological makeup, personality, and even sexual preferences as a result. Clarifying on sexual preferences here; Some Souls have been through traumatic experiences either in past lives or this life which can colorize the orientation of the current life movie patterns.

Souls incarnate within different patterns of male/female orientation which causes and allows for different sexual orientations including heterosexuality, homosexuality, and bi-sexuality. Not to judge anyone for being any certain way. Part of why we're here is to know and understand why we are the way we are. Some of us arrive with these patterns naturally, which can be remembered preferences from a past life, whether male or female. Some of us have endured traumas whether in past life or this life. Often in our current culture this occurs in childhood. The subconscious protocol is to block it out of the memory in order to keep going and living life. Often times I find that people who have unique orientations can have unique creativity and energy healing gifts.

Different families have different or unique patterns of interaction all coming through the DNA from the ancestors. Most often we see the influences in us from what our parents went through. This has been for much of society an Achilles's heal or stumbling block. Though it can be a great learning curve and healing tool once we decide to reflect, inspect, accept, forgive and release the past.

How did we arrive at the point of reference we're now at? Are we still evolving or have we reached a plateau where we live, love and experience continually in harmony? These are some of the questions that we ask ourselves when we check in to take inventory of our life and our path. We all seek to continually know ourselves personally and within the world in each moment while we are here. All of us at some point in our lives seek a sense of completion, peace and feeling like we've accomplished things that make us feel good.

As we correlate the dynamics available in the

Akashic Records with ancestral healing, we can achieve many unique healing qualities and gifts from this perspective. The Akashic Records and your Book of Life within them is linked directly to your Soul energy. In this way we can look at the effects of the events that we've been through in life and read into them. What is the greater lesson? What is the karma or 'cause and effect' that's involved with the life events?

As we process these thoughts we get insights that we're able to use practically for moving forward in our lives. We can see a challenging dynamic or a malady, what it may be tied to and how to unwind or release it. This can come in different ways. We can receive direct messages about events and how to clear our challenges with a certain event whether energetically or by receiving steps to heal by and live by.

The other dynamic which we will be referring back to in multiple ways over the course of this material is a Soul energy dynamic that hasn't been discussed since ancient times. As we look into the Records during a meditation at the events that have occurred we're looking for answers and clues, or building a case so to speak. Your Soul energy is active and connected to your past lives and to your Book of Life while this is occurring.

As you watch the movie of the current or past life event while keeping yourself calm and just continuing to view. The event is being brought to the surface of the consciousness as the Soul assimilates and soothes, heals and reintegrates your Total Self just by observing. You must remain calm though in order for it to assimilate and release. The normal mode of the monkey mind wants to come out of the vision and to start mentally trying to figure out how to fix what happened and the affects of it all.

Just by looking at the event while connected through the Soul energy is enough to clear and release the aftermath of any trauma. Once the trauma has been identified by the consciousness, the mind and the Soul while connected to the physical body can observe, assimilate and simply release any event by recognizing it. This is a very helpful dynamic when it comes to family healing and childhood healing, relationship healing or blocks of any type for that matter.

This is an ancient insight about the Akashic Records, the Book of Life and a person's Soul energy that has been long hidden and often communicated orally from teacher to adept throughout history. These subtle dynamics equal big shifts for releasing, clearing, healing, becoming enlightened and leading a normal healthy and functional life.

Our ancestors and family bloodline often can be in need of healing and clearing. When we are able to heal and clear our heritage we can be set free and moved forward sometimes like a springboard effect. At the very least you will receive hidden levels of healing, comfort and a positive feeling of moving freely forward. This can be done by looking at the complete bloodline en mass or by looking at or searching for specific defining events by individuals in our family tree that have had a trans-migrational effect through our genes and our DNA.

When you start to work on yourself or with others through acknowledging this observational view it can be enlightening to say the least. You may go through thoughts of wanting to be disconnected from all of them or maybe your family. You may immediately or after a while experience a healing that allows you to be with your family or to communicate with them without feeling hurt, lost or at a deficit. If you are fine with your immediate family there are almost always members of the ancestral family tree that could benefit from receiving healing. In the next exercise we will commence a family bloodline healing guided visualization from within the Akashic Records.

Exercise 3

Window through Eternity Healing the Family Tree

*Read the Script
and then practice your self guided visualization.*

This is a guided meditation for healing your family history. Just get comfortable and start to relax finding a place to sit, recline or lay down. If you are laying down a light blanket to cover the body can be very helpful. And a pillow under the knees.

I recommend having a glass of water within reach. As you start to get comfortable start to take some long slow deep breaths and close your eyes. Just continue to breathe in and out long and slow. As you continue to relax down your whole body becomes loose and limp and lazy. And as you relax now your toes, ankles and feet. Relaxing now your shins and calves, and your knees. Relaxing the space behind the knees. Relaxing your thighs and hamstrings. Your hips, waist and pelvis are all completely relaxed. As you relax down,

down even deeper, breathing long slow and relaxed breaths. Your lower stomach and lower back are all completely relaxed as the relaxing energy now moves up your spine to soothe your whole back.

As you continue to relax your torso and chest all completely relaxed. Make sure your shoulders are dropped and relaxed. Relaxing now your neck as you relax down, down, down even deeper. Releasing all the concerns of the day and the world, Relax your head and your eyes. Relax your face, and your cheeks, your ears are completely relaxed. Continuing to relax deeper and releasing all stress.

As you continue to relax you start to see coming into focus now a beautiful soft light from over head. As this light comes down around you it creates a beautiful golden portal that is filled with soft gold and white light.

Let the light come down around you and fill the room as it forms a great portal around you. This portal is full of soft white and gold healing light. As it grows slowly brighter everything in the room becomes a bit dimmer and fades back. As you are now in this light it starts to summon you upwards as your body becomes light like a feather.

As you start floating now up, up and away. As you float up through the ceiling and up through the sky now seeing all of the stars and celestial bodies as you float up through the white puffy clouds. And as you float up through the clouds the golden portal of light carries you gently. As you come up through the clouds you find yourself in a great hall. This great hall is very open and spacious with a tall arched ceiling.

As you look to the other end of the hall there is a very large picture window. Through this picture window you can see the Source Light of Eternity, The Essence of Creator God of Love. On each side of the great window is a door. To your left is also a door and to your right is another door on the sides of the hall.

As the left door now opens someone very special walks in. It is your **Child Self**, your beautiful Little One. Just take a moment to look at their features. Notice how special your little one is. So beautiful, gentle and pure. As they walk over to your left side looking up in your eyes and smiling and now taking your left hand. They are so happy to be here with you.

As the right door now opens someone else very special walks in. It is your Higher Self, your Perfect Self from the Perfect Universe. This powerful Light Being of which you came from moves closer to you. Touching your right hand you are now complete in the moment. These three parts of you are now integrated. Your Child Self, Your Adult Self and your Angelic Self. Your Subconscious, Conscious and Super-Conscious Self. Your **Past, Present and Future Self**. All merging here together.

Up ahead to the left of the picture window the door on the right now opens and in walks your mother. She is very radiant in her spiritual body here within the

Akashic Hall of Records. As she walks over to you she comes to stand across from you with some distance between you and her.

Next the door on the right opens and in walks your father. As he walks across the room smiling and comes to stand across from you on the right of your mother. He is very radiant in his light body and so happy to be here with you in the Great Hall.

You now raise hands as your Little One and Your Higher Self also raise their hands you start projecting powerful healing Love from your hands and your heart as you continue to project these healing streams. Notice the colors of the healing energies.

Emerald green, beautiful gold, soft magenta, and a brilliant blue. The energy is moving into the hearts of your mother and father. Now behind them starts to appear a great line of the family ancestors.

Your grandmothers and grandfathers. Your great grandmothers and great grandfathers. Your great, great grandmothers and great, great grandfathers and so on and so forth. And as the ancestors continue to appear in a long line they are lining up all the way out the picture window and back into the Source Light of God.

As you continue to broadcast this powerful healing energy through the hearts of your Mother and Father it moves through them healing, blessing and clearing them. Moving now through the hearts of your family line as it moves all the back through the generations.

ANCESTRAL HEALING EXERCISE

They are all lined up here for the healing that is good for their Soul.

As the energy moves through them it clears and heals any and all ailments or dis-eases that have been transmitted through the DNA. It also heals and clears any and all past generational karma that may have been coming forward through the ancestry. Emotional issues, prosperity issues, self worth issues, habitual tendencies. Correcting now the immune system, the nervous system, the cardiovascular system as they are all healed balanced and energized. Correcting the brain functions and the energy fields associated with the third eye and crown chakras. All is made well and whole as the powerful healing stream continues to flow through them.

As it flows all the way back through the ancient ancestors it finally reaches the Source Light of creation. As God feels the Healing Love being sent through the family tree there is an explosion of Love that God sends back through them forward from the ancient ancestors all the way forward in time to reach you.

As you see the healing energy coming closer from a great distance. As it comes closer coming into and through the hearts of your great, great grandmothers and great, great grandfathers. Through the hearts of your great grandmothers and great grandfathers. And your grandmothers and grandfathers and back through the hearts of your mother and father and back to You, your **Inner Child** and your **Higher Self**. Healing, clearing, balancing on every level. Correcting all generational karma, and healing the family DNA all done with LOVE.

As the energy is streaming from your hands continually now all the way through the lineage to God and then simultaneously coming back through the lineage all the way to You. The healing energy is moving in both directions along the time line. Both forward through time and back through time simultaneously. This is a form of Quantum Time Line Healing.

Your mother and father are very happy to see you and your inner child and to receive healing. As the stream softly completes itself the ancestors now start fading back through the picture window into the Source Light of Creation. And as your mother and father are so happy and thankful they both come forward and give you and your little one a loving hug. As they say their goodbyes and wishing you well, they walk back across the hall and move back through the doors on the left and right sides of the picture window.

Your Inner Child and your Higher Self are very happy they could assist you in this clearing and healing process. As you healed the family lineage the energy travelling through the ancient ancestors all the way back to God and then the energy travelling back from God through them again and back to You. Healing and balancing You your whole generational family lineage in every way.

Ancestral Healing Exercise

Your Little One tugs at your hand as you pick them up and they lay their head on your chest. They begin to fade into your heart, where they will always be with you, nurturing you and guiding you. As your Higher Self now touches your shoulders and downloads healing, strength, prosperity, love, joy, and a full spectrum of nutrients for your DNA and your cells.

Thanking your Angelic Self they now fade and become transparent light as they take their place standing behind you as your guide. There has been so much healing and clearing for you today to move you forward. Giving thanks to God and the Akashic Records knowing that you can come here anytime you wish as often as you wish for healing and self study. The Great Golden Portal of Light now appears again as it summons you to step into the middle of the stream.

As you do you feel yourself gently being moved back down through the ethers. Through the clouds back down through the skies. As you see the Earth coming closer and you now see your country coming closer. And you see your town as you come back down to and in through the ceiling and back into your body. Just take a few moments to integrate and come back into your body more fully. As you wiggle your toes and fingers, take a deep breath and let your Soul reintegrate with your body.

Thank You Divine Creator for overseeing this Healing of my Ancestors. Thank You Ancestors for being present to receive healing. And to my Higher Self from the Perfect Universe, please continue to guide me along with my Spirit Guides, Angels and Creator God.

Om Peace, Amen.

Hand position or Nasagra mudra for the Nadi Shodhana Alternate Nostril Breathing.

Exercise 4

ALTERNATE NOSTRIL BREATHING

This is a breathing meditation practice. The formal name is **Nadi Shodhana Pranayama**. Energy is running through the **Nadis** or energy pathways which lay along both sides of the spine from the tailbone all the way up the back of the head. In meditative visualization these pathways travel up the back of the head and meet up around the front of the crown like a halo around the forehead. These Nadis coincide with the spinal fluid which is running up and down along the spinal column and up around each side of the head and through the brain.

The term *Nadi* means 'channel' or 'flow of energy' and the term *Shodhana* means 'purification'. So Nadi Shodhana purifies the energy or pranic channels in the body. There are 2 main channels that run along the spine. The **Ida** and the **Pingala**.

The Ida channel in the spinal fluid on the left side of the spine is associated with the right side of the brain and the left side of the body bringing cooling and calming representing a softer more feminine energy.

The Pingala channel in the spinal fluid on the left side of the spine is associated with the right side of the body in unison with the left side of the brain is known for heating and activating the body. So whether you are active or calm the coinciding side of the brain and that nadi is more active or prominent. The practice of Alternate Nostril Breathing or the Nadi Shodhana will bring balance to your whole being. This is an excellent practice to use prior to going into an Akashic Records meditation or guided journey.

As you sit comfortably before practicing, place your first finger under your nose horizontally and check which nostril has more wind on the finger. If the left nostril has more wind this is the Ida nadi or pathway (right brain/left side of the body/cooling and calming) If the right nostril has more wind this is the Pingala Nadi (left brain/right side of the body/ heating and activating).

Note: *traditional Aryavedic studies recommend not to practice this pranayam technique if a person has a cold, flu or fever.*

In this breathing practice you will use the right hand in a hand position called the **Nasagra mudra**. The index and middle fingers are resting gently on the 3rd eye center between the eye brows. Place the thumb above the right nostril and the ring finger above the left nostril to control the flow of breath in the nostrils.

Exercise 3

The little finger can be relaxed.

Before you start, as a warm up exercise close your eyes and just take a 5 long slow inhales and exhales through both nostrils. Next:

1. Raise the right hand into position for the Nasagra mudra and close the right nostril with the thumb.
2. Inhale and exhale through the left nostril 5 times.
3. Then release the Right nostril and close the Left nostril with your ring finger.
4. Repeat the same thing. Inhale and exhale through the Right nostril 5 times.

When you have completed this cycle remove your hand and breathe normally 5 times through both nostrils.

And now comes the alternate nostril breathing:

1. Using the hand position (Nasagra mudra) touch the 3rd eye with the first 2 fingers of the right hand.
2. Close the Right nostril with the thumb and inhale long and slow through the Left nostril.
3. Release the Right nostril and close the Left nostril exhaling from the Right nostril.
4. Inhale from the Right nostril while closing the Left Nostril.
5. Exhale from the Left nostril while closing the Right nostril.

This is one round. Complete 5 rounds.

Once you are done return to 5 long slow breaths through both nostrils.

The benefits or Nadi Shodhana alternate nostril breathing or pranayama is to balance both hemispheres of the brain and to balance the nervous system. It will relieve stress, anger and anxiety. It can increase mental calmness and decrease blood pressure. It is also helpful for conditions such as bronchitis and asthma.

As we utilize this technique this helps to turn on the vision centers in the mind and allows you to glide through your Akashic Records visionary experience more effortlessly. It will help you to get into a comfortable and inter connected space more easily right before your Akashic meditation.

As you are starting the process and the left/right nostril breathing, Familiarize yourself with the Ida and the Pingala nadis or pathways and which sides of the brain, spine and body they coincide with. This will help your mind to naturally assimilate and become more aware of the nervous system itself. As you continue through time you may even be able to sense and autonomically control the flow of the Ida and Pingala nadis by focusing on them with intention. That is another practice, we'll revisit in the Advanced material. For now become familiar with the left and right sides and the cross connections with the brain hemispheres and the body.

Benefits of Nadi Shodhana Alternate Nostril Breathing:

- It brings the mind to the present moment and out

Exercise 3

of the past which helps to release old fears, regret and worry, calming the mind.
- Beneficially Therapeutic for the Respiratory, Cardiovascular, and Nervous systems.
- Relieves stress, tension and anxiety.
- This harmonizes the left and right hemispheres of the brain, which correlate to the logical and the emotional sides of our personality.
- Helps to purify and balance the Nadis (the subtle energy channels) ensuring smooth flow of pranic life force through the body.
- Helps maintain the body temperature.

AS YOU JOURNEY UP INTO THE AKASHIC RECORDS WHILE HOLDING THE CRYSTALS AS AMPLIFIERS YOU MAY CONNECT THROUGH YOUR MIND AND SENSES DIRECTLY INTO THE RECORDS.

Chapter 11
Using Crystals to Access the Records

As you keep expanding, growing and diving deeper into your intuitive studies and the Akashic Records, you may at some point have had inclinations to explore the world of gem stones and minerals. This can be a very intuitively guided link or connection for you.

I continued to work with the Akashic Records from my early findings of it along with Yoga, and different forms of energy work and healing. As I started to work more and more with individuals and groups in public settings or in personal guidance and healing sessions, I was very soon shown to seek extra help from the world of minerals and crystals as a direct way of keeping my energy clear and protected. Depending on where I was located the energy could be up or down and my personal spiritual energy had not yet opened to the current levels where it's easier to navigate the varying energies naturally. It is a learning and unfolding process as the energy fields in and around your body continue to ebb and flow as you grow, release and expand.

I knew that I had ample energy to draw from as I continued to work, though I often dipped into my personal reserves without actually knowing or intending to. Maybe at times I did know that I was leaking energy but I was more intent on helping the person I was working with heal in the moment. This is where the aid of the crystals really came into play. Spirit, the Universe, Living Reality and my Guides were revealing a synchronous relationship that would continue to grow for years to come.

The first minerals that I worked with were for protection, clearing and healing. A large chunk of Selenite sat between myself and the participants at readings that I would lay my hands across to hold theirs as I connected with their Records. I also used a large bundle of Sage. The other minerals that I remember using earlier were common. Rose Quartz for healing, soothing and clearing and Amethyst for clearing and connecting to the Higher Mind and Soul energy. Orange Calcite for soothing and bringing a person's core energy levels back up. Citrine for clearing, opening the mind and manifesting. And a few more which I'll go into detail later in this chapter.

Edgar Cayce made a statement at one time in his

Using Crystals to access the Records

life and even named a book after it...'There is a River'. These are very profound words that I will be using from time to time to describe the streams of energy. The more you work with a crystal the more interactive it will become with your energy. It will be like a field, stream or a river that you step into. As you ebb and flow it will move with your energy. You may not feel it at all when you start and that is perfectly normal. You may feel subtle energy that will open over time. Or you may feel the full on energy connection with the stone from the start.

When you start to work with crystals it can be an interactive and growing experience. Often times many of us go to the shows or the stores and buy crystals and we bring them home and set them around the house. This is always a good thing because they are able to work with your energy subtly by osmosis. Often many people on some level know there is more but they never get past buying them, taking them home and putting them on a window sill or shelf.

You have to pick them up and hold them. Spend time listening to the frequency with your own energy and body. How does each one make you feel? As you read about the properties choose one or more references to learn from. The 'Book of Stones' is an extensive classic but there are many others and scads of info on the internet. This comes in handy if you're in front of some stones that you're feeling a particular vibration from and need to know more about it. You can often do a search online from your phone in the moment and find enough information to quickly let you know if the properties of that mineral or that particular gem stone are something that you need to work with.

It will turn into a life long study and relationship if you let it. Learning slowly as you go along steadily is the best way. Gathering a stone or crystal here or there as you feel guided. When you first start reading about the properties of each stone, don't feel overwhelmed. I say that because you're more than likely going to. It may seem that every crystal does everything and you need them all!

As you read the simple definitions that may come with each stone they can be more generalized, overlapping and run together. It was challenging for me to make heads or tails out of everything starting out because of the vast number of different stones and minerals available.

It does become much easier once you start having the experience of feeling what the energy is doing with yours. Once you start having those references and interactions you're off to the races...or to the gem store should I say. The simple definitions will make more sense as you come to feel the stones in order to know what the strength and the depth of the interactive connection will be for you at that time. Much like entering the Records it's an intuitively guided process.

Using Crystals to Access the Records

When I connect into the Akashic Records for someone and read from their Book of Life for them I usually like to use a matched set of Red Lemurian crystals that I've been using for a long time. For me I usually find that Red, Pink, Tangerine and Yellow Lemurian crystals from Brazil or that area work very well for reading the Akashic Records.

There may be many people selling gem stones that continue to pass along the same nick names or definitions of a stone in order to sell in the moment. Some folks will know more than others. Just ask for guidance when looking for the right stones and crystals for you. You may have heard the term 'record keeper'. Sometimes the crystals really are 'record keepers' and sometimes they're using that term to sell product. You be the judge with each stone. You don't *have* to buy anything. Only get what you are guided to. Just remember they may all be calling your name!

I like to recommend to my students a simple matched pair of reading crystals to start reading with. One for each hand. I will have these available for you in the classes and at my site or you can find your own. Another tip is that I usually find clear quartz crystals are an amplifier for anything else around them, that is why I prefer the tinted Lemurians. They have a unique vibration that will work well with just about anyone's energy and the deep vibration coming from the Living Library of the Earth itself.

As you journey up into the Akashic Records while

holding the crystals as amplifiers you may connect through your mind and senses directly into the Records. Another way to connect is to ask the Crystals that you are holding to connect into the Records and let the energy come directly through them to you, so they may speak messages as well. As always, trust your vision, thoughts and mind messages coming through in the moments. Allow your Self to receive as you experience and move beyond the thoughts or doubts that you might be making it all up in your own mind. That is key.

I now want to go over a list of Crystals that I think are beneficial and important to have in your work.

One of the main keys to working with hand held crystals for the purpose of healing or intuitive reading is to find the way that the crystal best sits into the palm of your hand. Move it around in multiple positions. You will usually find a certain position or way that the stone wants to be held in. Sometimes there can be indentations or ridges that fit just perfectly for your fingers and thumbs to be placed into.

You will know what I'm talking about after you experiment and experience this. You will find yourself able to spot these stones and crystals easily upon your initial examination of them. To someone else it might just be a rough stone, irregular or unpolished. To You though it is a powerful intuitive and healing tool just waiting to bring amazing added qualities to your personal work and work with others!

Using Crystals to access the Records

A List of Some Crystals and their Benefits

Rose Quartz - Healing and clearing, and has a very soft energy. Good for everything and everyone. Clearing in the Heart, emotions and home. Associated with Quan Yin.

Amethyst - Healing and clearing. Works with the crown chakra. Violet energy is beneficial for clearing and protecting everything and everyone. Associated with St. Germain.

Lemurian Crystals - Lemurian Crystals help you to feel connected to the soft, loving energies of the celestial realms. The ladder-like striations on this stone act as a "stairway to heaven" and reaches towards higher frequencies. They are powerful meditation tools which bring a feeling of temporarily coming home for those who feel isolated, lonely or that the earth is not their home. Good for reading the Akashic Records.

Citrine - Enhances mental clarity and allows for the flow of ideas and visualizing. Especially when used in meditation. Very effective in strengthening mental output and establishing goals. Citrine is associated with the root, sacral and solar plexus chakras. By connecting with the sacral chakra, the citrine healing properties are most effective in stimulating an increase in sexual and creative fertility. The conception of both ideas and life can be plentiful under citrine's power to motivate. It also links to the root chakra to bring the physical energy up to the emotional (solar plexus), and raise all energy to a higher plane. Citrine can be helpful to clear the blocks in the root chakra. The solar plexus is the central energy distributor, and citrine's connection to this chakra will elevate energy levels and general circulation.

Black Tourmaline - One of the most powerful minerals for absorbing electromagnetic radiation, which makes it excellent for placing near computers and other electronics. It is self clearing and one the best self protection and clearing stones. I recommend having this on your night stand, in your car and possibly even carrying a small piece with you in your pocket.

Blue Agate - Very cooling and calming stone, endowing us with a sense of peace and tranquillity. A powerful throat healer, it assists with verbal expression of thoughts and feelings. It is a great nurturing and supportive stone, neutralizing anger, infection, inflammation and fever.

Blue Lace Agate helps to strengthen and accelerate the repair of bones, thyroid deficiencies, throat and lymph infections. It soothes red, sore eyes and any skin problems associated with redness and irritation.

Calcite (all colors) - Open and recharge your chakras with the Calcite crystals. They are very comforting for the soul. Made up of calcium carbonate, the Calcite crystal meaning has a reputation for being a great energy amplifier. Each variety also has its own distinctive properties that provide rich and soulful nutrition necessary for creativity and spiritual insight to flourish.

Green Calcite promotes healing, prosperity and good fortune, and Orange Calcite, a radiant stone that harnesses the energy of the sun and its life-giving power that turns night into day. Also available are Red, Blue and Yellow. Please research their unique and distinctive properties. Calcite is another good stone to have close by while you sleep. Also good for rebuilding one's core energy.

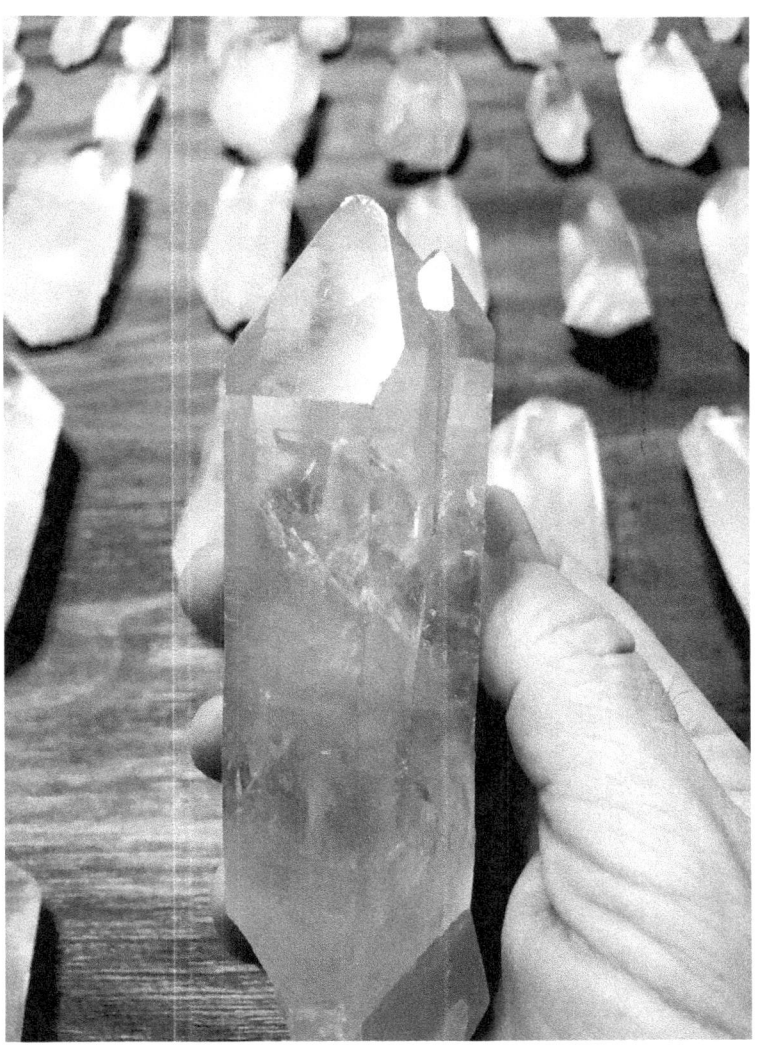

Chapter 12
Earth Portals To The Records

*I*n truth there are many ways to access the Akashic Records. In my personal experience from this life and beyond in the 'in between' while working in the Records between lifetimes and past lives, there are several perspectives that can continue to be helpful for your personal practice.

As you experience the exercises and practice the meditations towards gaining access and entry into your own Book of Life and the Akashic Records, you will be gaining valuable intricate and subtle insights, aspects and techniques which will add wisdom and foundation to your studies.

In our primary journeys into the Akasha we practice tending our mind straight up through the ethers and into the outer layers of earth's atmosphere. This is where we can more easily access the higher dimensions where the true Records are stored. We learn in this portion of the work about the dynamics of our Soul and how we are connected simultaneously into our own Book of Lifetimes within the Akasha. We also learn how to journey up and out, while similar to astral travel, though with a 'target location' to travel to. We gather information through visual, audio and sentient remote dream experiences and then we return to our body and we reintegrate as we process the knowledge that we've just gathered. Hopefully this brings you closer to knowing your true nature and essence.

Moving up and out of the body to experience within the higher dimensional home of the Records is a primary way of studying these heavenly streams of information, knowledge and data. And now we bring to You another primary way of accessing in another deeply unique technique. Through the Earth.

The Earth has a whole unique set of special dynamics to teach you about accessing her etheric memory banks. As we travel up into the Akashic Records in the outer atmosphere of the Earth we go into higher dimensional, heavenly qualities of the Akasha which are more etheric and air-like. For all practical purposes this is Step 1 in tending to access correctly. Aligning the intellect, the mind, conscious awareness with your own Soul and it's streaming connection up into your personal Book of Life within the Records.

The next way to access which we will explore is by tending or directing the mind deep down into the Earth. There there are special levels or information

Earth Portals Into the Records

here which are different in nature. In some ways more personal to the physical body where the cellular memory is kept. The body has within it hidden pathways through it's tissue to other times where imprints were made and stored. Often this is a way in which we can identify traumas of past lives or from childhood. Times and places in which we somehow held onto something with the body for the purpose of either colorful conditioning through our personal filters or hidden and stored away for future processing and release.

The challenging dynamic that most people are faced with when trauma from the body surfaces or resurfaces is that the ego tries to hang onto it through fear, survival or 'fight or flight' mode. As the memories and bodily sensation arise in certain areas, the body remembers instances where it may have been fighting for it's own life whether, physically, mentally or emotionally. This is local time looping in the body.

The ego through it's preconditioned work ethic has a continual tendency naturally to take these traumas from the body and attempt to pull them back down into the deep hidden layers of the mind and body in hopes of managing the survival and balance of the complete individual. Even to the extent of sometimes blocking events or parts of a person's life from their memory which are deemed too painful to reexperience even in regular memories.

Could we consider for a moment in time that when this is occurring it is actually a gift that is being given to us to use for our personal healing in the moment? The release is like enlightenment or ascension for the body tissue. As the issues come up and are experienced, the decision in the moment by conscious choice to move forward by staying present with the feelings and memories and to Release them in that moment is all that's needed.

Making an effort to pushing forward in the balance of the moment by not caving in to letting the cellular memories become buried again, but staying present in balance while focusing on the 'gift' of the perceptual memory in order to release it from the body and give it back to the Universe or God to be recycled as pure energy.

The Earth can transmute these energies from a person as well by pulling it deep down into the earth and recycling them into pure energy. So look at the 'Gift' that the tissue of the body, the emotional self and the mind can receive by being present to this work. Through release of the contractions into expansion these parts that make up the Self can receive sentient enlightenment or ascension like qualities of release, comfort, peace and healing!

By travelling downwards into the caves of the Earth and connecting with our own personal Books of Life there, we start to look into a more elemental and even more Earthy side to these

Records. For some it could be similar to travelling upwards into the Records. For others it can be completely different. The key is to remain calm and continue to view and experience without becoming emotionally activated through the ego.

The Earth through it's elemental pathways has deep hidden nurturing layers to teach us about. Things about ourselves that are sometimes so close that we cannot usually look into them or process them as part of our immediate personal perception.

We may also feel as part of a deep connection with the living, breathing mother Earth what is connected to her. What is going on and what is she experiencing and/or feeling. Another element to the unique qualities to be considered are that of the lay lines of the earth and earth vortexes. The Earth is changing as we step into the New Age and move through photonic light field in space. As our local sun's energy increases, all of these dynamics cause the Earth's usual patterns that cause certain places to feel a certain way all to shift or to move. Locations that once felt good to us can now feel either too intense or lower in vibration. Locations that once felt varied or lower can now seem more comfortable. This can also happen naturally for an individual as their own energy shifts and changes. So the key here is that energy will somewhat be shifting both within you and in the physical world as you proceed. Stop, look, listen and then proceed. You will find your way. Namaste.

Exercise 5

Journey into the Earth Records

*Read the Script
and then practice your self guided visualization.*

This is a guided meditation into your own personalized Book of Life set within the Earth Records. Just get comfortable and start to relax finding a place to sit, recline, lay down and get comfortable. If you are laying down with a light blanket to cover the body can help the body to feel safe as you journey. Also a pillow under the knees to relax your back. I recommend having a glass of water within reach. As you start to get comfortable start to take some long slow deep breaths and close your eyes.

Just continue to breathe in and out long and slow. As you continue to relax down your whole body becomes loose and limp and lazy. And as you relax now your toes, ankles and feet. Relaxing now your shins and calves, and your knees. Relaxing the space behind the knees. Relaxing your thighs and hamstrings. Your hips, waist and pelvis are all completely relaxed. As you relax down, down even deeper, breathing long slow and relaxed breaths. Your lower stomach and lower back are all completely relaxed as the relaxing energy now moves up your spine to soothe your whole back. As you continue to relax your torso and chest all completely relaxed.

Make sure your shoulders are dropped and relaxed. Relaxing now your neck as you relax down, down, down even deeper. Releasing all the concerns of the day and the world, Relax your head and your eyes. Relax your face, and your cheeks, your ears are completely relaxed. Continuing to relax deeper and releasing all stress.

As you continue to Relax down even deeper, find yourself now in a beautiful nature setting. As you're here see a natural gently winding path that wraps around the right side of a continual gradual hill. As you see the green grass and the trees. There are birds singing in the background and a gentle breeze you can feel blowing your hair and touching your skin. As you see the late afternoon sun up ahead, the golden light is warming your face and body as you walk along the gently winding path in the direction of the sun.

Continuing to walk you now find to your left the entrance of a cave. And as you move in closer to investigate there are some steps carved from the earth that lead down to a great wooden door.

As you open the door you see a very old message on the wall that reads

"May This Door be Opened to All Who Enter."

You see that there is a level walkway made from the earth that moves gradually down into the distance. As you take a few steps there is a wall torch that is immediately illuminated by a soft golden light.

As you continue your journey down into the deep earth path the wall torches continue to be lit with a golden light for you. This lets you feel that you are being welcomed. That there is something for you to be shown or to find.

Continuing eventually the path and tunnel starts winding down to the left in wide spiralling patterns. As you continue the torches shine with a violet light that you move through. Continuing forward there is now a deep indigo light that you walk through. As the spiral continues you now are immersed in a bright blue as you walk down along the spiralling walkway. The torches now blaze with a beautiful emerald green. Moving down through the tunnel the light now changes to a soft golden essence. Changing now to a bright orange as you spiral down, down and away and now moving through a deep ruby red light. The spiral now comes to a set of ancient wooden double doors.

As you open the doors, you are met by a very large cavern of immensity. This cavern has a natural sky light which shows you the heavens. You also are also looking out across the sea and there are waterfalls here within the great earth room. A truly natural and mystical place that you have found. As you look around at the cave walls you notice that there are tapestries. These tapestries are in the air and are holographic. They run around the band of your head but extended out between you and the cave walls.

As you notice the 360 degree nature of the tapestries, the directional expansion allows your mind to creatively expand into the visions contained within the tapestries. As you scan them you choose one to focus into. Now viewing the moving pictures of the tapestry, it starts to tell you a story about your lives. Maybe a specific past life or other time line where you have experienced another life's movie.

The essence of the vision is speaking to you from deep within. Telling you a story. Just allow the story to unfold as you watch the movie.

After a while you look around and you find in the center of the great natural Earth Hall a rock platform which is holding a very large and ancient book. As you move closer to the book you notice that there are symbols forming now before your eyes that are bringing a deep feeling of connection for you. Some symbols that you're seeing for the first time and some symbols that seem familiar. They are moving and alive as they animate themselves in the book. Look into the moment and just be with them. Allow them to continue coming into your mind's eye.

As you reach out in front of you placing now your hands on both pages of this ancient book. Your finger tips are seeing and feeling as your nervous system and your inner vision also connects directly with your personal book of Earth Records. The Book of Your Soul's History and how you came to be. Continue to look at the Book and sense the nature of the pages. As you look deeper into the Book you now start to turn the great pages with your hands feeling the large thick pages. As you stop at another place in the book there are more messages for you here. Take a few moments to look into this Great Book of your Lifetimes and receive messages, pictures and images..

Looking up from the book now around the room at the cave walls you notice that there are patterns of symbols and written messages. They are moving up out of the stone and then back into the stone like living waves of information. Take a few moments to read or connect with these living breathing written messages.

As you look up now across the great room out through the skylight at the sea. You feel a sense of being gratified with what you have received, found, been given and shown here. As you walk out toward the natural skylight and sea, you find yourself outside the cave and now see the earthen path which winds back around the hill. This leads you back to the path along which you started in the beautiful nature setting. As you now come right back into the present moment and the waking state. Opening your eyes, moving your fingers and toes and take a few deep breaths.

Please take a few moments to journal and write down or draw anything you might have seen. Do not worry about the level of your artistic abilities, your mind will remember how to get back to your visions from what you write down or draw. Enjoy the process.

Journey Into the Earth Records

True perception of the Self is your best friend. This gives you self acceptance. When you accept yourself completely your perception of everything changes for the better.

Chapter 13
Expanding Clearing Energizing & Grounding

One of the unique and sometimes seemingly unnoticed dynamics that can continually or sporadically occur is being unaware or 'asleep'. As we start to 'wake ourselves up' it is a continually changing process. We see ourselves through the inner mirror of our own reflection. Whether it be physical, mental, emotional, spiritual or all of the above.

Perhaps the world has kept us busy for a very long time. Coming and going from one situation to another. Family, work, weather, repairs, political, health, travel and many other situational experiences can keep us looping through the moments, hours, days, weeks, months or years and on to the next.

Until at some point we stop one day in front of the mirror and notice that we have changed. This is the mental mirror of perception. What have the years taught us to be through our responses to our life and the world around us?

Often times we stop and look in the mirror only to check for what's out of place or wrong with us, usually starting with our hair and face. Maybe the ego has us viewing our self through the eyes of denial. Afraid of it's own death the ego tends to keep us in a suspended state of animation from moment to moment to moment. Until either by chance or by intending a change in perception that we notice things about ourself that are peculiar or different.

Could it be that we're seeing ourself or the situational moment clearly for the first time? These moments of clarity can be great motivators for change in our lives. We are changing, growing and aging while many things around us (inanimate objects) and places remain the same. Our ego through our mind can still think and operate as if we are in a child like state of youth, while the body is full grown. There can be benefits or set backs to this depending on mental balance or the lack there of it.

True perception of the Self is your best friend. This gives you Self Acceptance. When you accept yourself completely your perception of everything changes for the better. We start to become more abundantly interactive with life. We are able to move through and let go of the past and welcome new people, places and things into our lives. If a person has been self absorbed in the lower levels of survival and comes into a clearer view of release and self healing, the

Energizing, Expanding & Clearing

outcomes can be nothing short of magical or a spiritual experience.

So as we release in many ways we are shifting more into perceptions of the present moment. Coming to fully perceive and accept the current moment and everything in it including our self. This allows for expansion of our personal energy. As we expand we come into contact with others and the external world in a new clear way. Within the expansion are opportunities for new situations, relationships, healing, creativity and prosperity. To enjoy the here and now completely.

In a lower way of perceiving, the ego and mind love to keep us looping through the unknown from moment to moment. It can become habitual and when this continues the subconscious mind starts to pay attention to the looping mysteries. This can conjure fear, indecision, uncertainty and a whole myriad of other emotional and energetic responses that are substandard to having a loving, healthy and prosperous life experience.

When you find yourself in these uncertain moments move into or allow a thought of trust or faith that the next moment, hours or days will be showing you a knowingly creative pathway to your fulfilment in life. This is a practice that takes practice. It will allow for your expansion to resolve itself. Your personal energy within and your energy fields have a tendency to expand and contract in reactions and responses to life. As you become more expanded continually your fields will naturally start to flow with more rhythmic tides of expansion and contraction. As the expansion continues your energy body will adjust and arrive at a more relaxed balance between the previous levels of guarded contraction and the **Universal Expansion of Cosmic Oneness**.

Clearing

As your complete self seeks change, one of the important factors to your personal spiritual growth and your work with energy itself will be the process of clearing. There are many different kinds of clearing. On a mundane level when we find ourselves in our surroundings at home being unable to navigate physically from one room or area to the next it's usually because of clutter. So whether happily or out of duress, we go to work to clean and clear a path. Often times for most of us we find that it is a challenge to think clearly when there is too much clutter in the external surroundings.

In much the same way we can start to slow down or become encumbered as we become layered with different kinds of energy that aren't really in our best interested to hold on to or to harbor. As we continue through our lives we operate as if the extra energies that we have been carrying are our own or that we have some sort of unspoken responsibility to them.

For those of us who are on our spiritual path of

Energizing, Expanding & Clearing

learning and healing as we become more aware we will at some point know that we need to release the old so that we can be in the Now more functionally and welcome the new.

Even as energy practitioners we sometimes neglect to do our own clearing while we continue to help others heal. This is like the age old story of the shoe maker with no shoes for his family. Whether sooner or later out of preventative maintenance or necessity you will seek energy clearing.

The most common way to quickly and functionally clear yourself is with a Native American smudge stick made of sage. A smudge stick is lit and burned as it is waved through your fields while you hold the intention for clearing and release. The smoke of the burning sage is what does the work to clear any negative or lower energies in your body's fields, your surroundings or your home.

Other forms of clearing include using sea salt in your home. Sea salt is often placed at the entrance of a home and/or in the corners of the rooms. Sea salt in a bath can be very relaxing, therapeutic and clearing. Essential oils such as lavender, sage, patchouli and frankincense can also be very helpful in clearing.

Prayers and affirmations are key in releasing negative energies as you are asking God, the Universe, the healers on the other side and your guides to remove that which is not serving you.

Sometimes a more in depth form of clearing

is needed such as **Shamanic Soul Retrieval**, Soul healing or a house clearing and blessing. Shamanism is an ancient tribal practice of working with the earth's energy and the animal familiars (spirits) to bring back a person's Soul energy to them which was trapped in time and to release any things that have been tagging along with them whether elemental energy, another person's energy or a non-physical being which has attached to them for some reason or another.

Another way to clear yourself and your surroundings is with the aid of crystals or minerals. Rose quartz commonly known for it's heart based energy is also a good stone to keep you and your space clear. Black Tourmaline is an excellent protective stone for clearing. Amethyst, Obsidian, Shungite, Agate and many others can be used for the purpose of protection and clearing.

As you continue your journey in life of self knowing and understanding you may become sensitive to energy or your inner and outer world. This is a time when you will most generally be sensitive to what feels good and what doesn't.

This may be associated to energy sources that need to be cleared from you and situations you may be or have been involved with which need reconciliation. As you continue through life's processes you will become more accustomed to what feel's good and what doesn't.

Continual clearing maintenance will yield positive

results. It may seem like an inconvenience at times but the alternative of being encumbered by lower energies, that are not really your responsibility, can be much more difficult and time consuming. So practice clearing in whatever ways best speak to you. We often learn what works best through necessity.

Energizing

Energizing yourself with positive energy is one of the most beneficial things you can do. There are so many different ways to do this and so many benefits from it.

One of the most natural and common ways is through a healthy diet and getting ample amounts of rest, balanced with enough exercise to burn calories and stimulate your muscles, organs and systems of the body to flow with natural rejuvenating energy.

Another great way is to take up the practice of Tai Chi or Qi Gong. These are both great studies from traditional ancient energy practices. They will give you a great study on personal energy flow both in the body and around the body. I highly recommend these practices to anyone interested in studying energy healing.

Yoga will also be another way of energizing your body, mind and spirit. As you do the **asanas** or yogic postures which involve slow stretches and breath work you will find yourself utilizing yet another traditional practice which releases old stagnant energy and bringing in new fresh energy for your total self to process.

Meditation is an excellent way to release, let go and welcome fresh energy into your being. There are multiple different meditation techniques over the course of a lifetime. Find a style that speaks to you and stick with it as you explore other styles from time to time. There are many different meditation techniques in this material to explore, practice and utilize. Yogic breathing meditations, Zen techniques, walking meditation as well as many others. Using mandalas, mantras and mudras are more advanced and creative ways of cultivating energy. **Solar Gazing** can be a very unique practice to explore. Many masters from ancient times used solar gazing to increase their energy vibration. Please be careful and look up the suggested safety guidelines for the powerful practice of solar gazing. (only at sunrise and sunset)

Again crystals can be a great source of increasing personal energy. As you familiarize yourself with all of the different varieties of minerals, stones and crystals notice how they feel to you and how your personal energy interacts with them. Holding them in meditation with intention and also studying the specific benefits of each stone can be helpful in moving you forward in positive subtle and even profound ways.

You may also want to explore having energy healing sessions with a qualified practitioner. You will know what feels the best to you as you try different styles. Remember the old saying, 'Necessity is the mother of invention.' If you're feeling off in any way seek help. The best way to find the right energy practitioner of style of energy work is to intend it. Simply pray to God or ask the Universe to bring you help and to bring you back into alignment or to break old patterns and move forward. As you ask the way will be shown.

GROUNDING

Last but certainly not least is the practice of grounding. Grounding is so important. Anything that is electrical or runs on energy needs a clear direct ground in order to create and sustain energy. In the same manner we need grounding. After years of energy work, metaphysical and spiritual study if an individual feels 'out there' or ungrounded they could simply look at the dynamic of earth & sky, yin & yang, and expansion & grounding and it will be so helpful to take everything to a more significant level of clarity including the increased expansion that they've been seeking if they are willing to more deeply ground.

As we evolve, we tend to want to expand and increase energy flow, creativity, abundance, self knowing, wisdom and the list goes on.

Three things that are core and work well together:

A. Grounding
B. Water.
C. Ample Rest

These three things will functionally allow your personal energy system to continue to run and increase for you in a seamless and balanced way.

The enigma of the ego is that it wants to run faster and jump higher. It doesn't want to necessarily be grounded or held down. The secret that is hidden in plain sight is that if we ground we can easily run faster and jump higher with little or no exhaustion. You will even feel free to expand even more the deeper you ground.

There are many ways to ground. Getting enough sleep, a healthy diet and exercise are all more than enough to lead you forward in a balanced grounded way towards any intentions of spiritual expansion.

Here is a grounding exercise we use in the classes to make sure that we're all grounded. Use as needed:

Grounding Technique

If you ever feel light-headed, a bit woozy or tired after meditation or energy work, this will subside and disappear as your system becomes accustomed to the extra energy and oxygen. Take a moment to stretch your hands over your head, take a deep breath and while exhaling all the air out of your lungs, squatting down and touching the ground with both hands and make yourself 'heavy like a rock'. Feel yourself heavy like a rock. Become a rock. Let the Earth and Gravity have you. Repeat this 3 to 4 times. This will ground you.

Energizing, Expanding & Clearing

The hidden secret that is in plain sight is that if we ground we can easily run faster and jump higher with little or no exhaustion. You will even feel freer to expand even more the deeper you ground.

Trusting is the gateway between believing and knowing. Understanding the dynamics of believing, trusting, and knowing helps us to navigate through our mind's unique creative playground and add Faith to the whole process.

Chapter 14
BELIEVING TRUSTING & KNOWING

Believe - To accept something as true; feel sure of the truth of. • To accept the statement of someone as true. • To have faith, esp. religious or spiritual faith: • To believe something or someone. Feel sure that someone is capable of a particular action. • Yo hold (something) as an opinion; think or suppose.

Often to continue forward in life whether on a project or a state of mind that something is possible we start with belief. Believing in the possibility that something might exist or that we can achieve a goal is the beginning point of our journey. Our journey from that point forward whether life long or progressive may include belief systems, new ideas of creative thought or possibilities of manifestation for us are now part of our new personal world life movie. Belief in ourselves and in a true purpose for living is the core that all Souls in human form revolve around. And it is this central belief that manifests as many creative variations of belief systems through different civilizations, races and cultures. The key to our existence, survival, evolution and growth are all built on belief. Whether it be subtle, subconscious, recognized or even superstitious beliefs. It's what makes our worlds go round. Along with trust and knowing, belief is the incubator or fire starter of the mind, heart and soul that gives us the foundation to move about our reality with either presupposed idealisms or new ideas that can spawn evolving creative progress.

Every inventor has to harness the energy of believing whether openly, personally or subconsciously to move forward on their ideas in bringing them into fruition. Every researcher uses the energy of belief as they study lost civilizations and artifacts and come to reach a hypothesis about the nature of that age or part of the world.

Hope is a predetermining state that gives rise to the possibility of our beliefs bringing us forward into a better moment, condition or version of a healthy and prosperous life.

Anyone who has participated in a religious or spiritual group around the world incorporates belief into their studies and worship in order to achieve consistency and to move to new or higher levels spiritually.

BELIEVING, TRUSTING & KNOWING

Believing is the first step in actualizing a goal. Believing, Achieving and Receiving. In this material believing is the foundation for moving into the work. Learning about all of the aspects of the Akashic Records of which you are part of, and then studying the information and exercises to gain entry and access to these great banks of knowledge. If you've come this far you have either a burning desire or a curiosity about your Soul, the Akashic Records, your Book of Life, your Souls's Purpose and how it all works together. You have stirred thoughts and ideas within yourself that there is something more to your existence. I encourage you to continue and let your beliefs guide you into a faith that will then guide you towards knowing and understanding yourself which will create wisdom in your world.

Trust - Firm belief in the reliability, truth, ability, or strength of someone or something. • Acceptance of the truth of a statement without evidence or investigation. • The state of being responsible for someone or something. • A person or duty for which one has responsibility. • A hope or expectation.

So now you've come through your beliefs. You have worked with your beliefs within your self enough that they have come to a greater level or resonance for you. This greater level of belief we know now as Trust or Faith. Trust is the level that we have arrived at which is a bit smoother in the internal belief system. Trust allows us to put our beliefs on auto pilot and continue moving forward with grace and ease.

Trusting is the place that you have arrived at which affords you to relax the conscious mind and let life and the subconscious mind guide you through your journey. When you recognize this Trust within you and everything in life on your journey it becomes much easier, simpler, streamlined and flowing. When you have achieved a level of trust within yourself, you will let things unfold as they will knowing that life holds the answers to your creative inquiries.

Trusting is the gateway between believing and knowing. Understanding the dynamics of believing, trusting, and knowing helps us to navigate through our mind's unique creative work space and add Faith to the whole process. Trusting is the magic that gets you on to the next level. So trust, let go and let the Universe, your guides and God participate in overseeing your journey. Trust in yourself. Trust in the world to bring you what you need in life. Walk forward in the magic light of Trusting one step at a time.

In our Akashic studies we have believed in a place, space and dynamic which our Souls are interacting with. As we develop our techniques from within the Records we come to trust that we can achieve results in our studies with these dynamics. We trust our own ability to have a successful Akashic meditation. We trust that we are getting clear messages for our self and for others. We trust our ability to interpret the Records with grace and ease. We come to trust that there are benefits to our interaction with the Akashic Records that bring us to new levels of awareness in our lives.

Know - To be aware of through observation, inquiry, or information. • To have knowledge or information concerning. • To be absolutely certain or sure about something. • To have a good command of such as a subject or language. • To recognize someone or something. • To be familiar or acquainted with something. • To have personal experience of an emotion or situation. • To regard or perceive as having a specified characteristic. • To be able to distinguish one person or thing from another.

Once we have come from believing something's possible into trust that it will work for us, the next phase of integration is to know something as being part of our reality. When you know something to be true you have a steadfast belief and trust that it is working for you on your behalf and you develop a second nature foundation of thought around whatever it is that you are focusing on. A confidence in your perception.

When you know that you know you are right. The similarities between Belief, Trust and Knowing are subtle and sometimes overlapping. Knowing is a more ingrained way of trusting something to be true. It's a deeper level and at the same time a more effortless streaming of what works for you already and what you bring into your world through new alignments that works for you. Knowing starts to simplify the process of believing and trusting in the way that things in life simply work out and play out.

Knowing that something is working and streaming in your mind or reality is also knowing in a subtle way that you may pay less attention to it and let it move for you on it's own. Knowing something is the premise that it has already been accepted into your awareness. It has been processed and agreed upon whatever the coloration of that item, person, event, issue or place is.

Also to know something is to be aware of it. So you have looked at it, observed it and processed it through and through in your filtering lens of consciousness and come to accept it as a foundation.

In our work within the Akashic Records as we first find out about the Records we then move towards coming to believe that it is possible to look within them, or to believe that we have the possibility to know more. We then trust the process as we learn, study and apply the techniques for looking into these great banks of knowledge. We learn to trust ourselves and the process through doing the exercises and the meditations. We come to know ourselves more through the process of looking into our own Book of Lifetimes.

We also come to know that greater things are possible through reading our own Soul Records. Including Soul Healing, Karmic Release, Physical Healing, Manifesting a Better Life and the list goes on. Once we start knowing our selves at this level, so much more is possible for us including being more ready and fit for the coming afterlife and our appointment with eternity. We will have come to know that we have started the karmic cleanup process while still in body on this side of the veil as opposed to waiting until after we transition to start sorting it out. And we utilize the Akashic Records to do all of this!

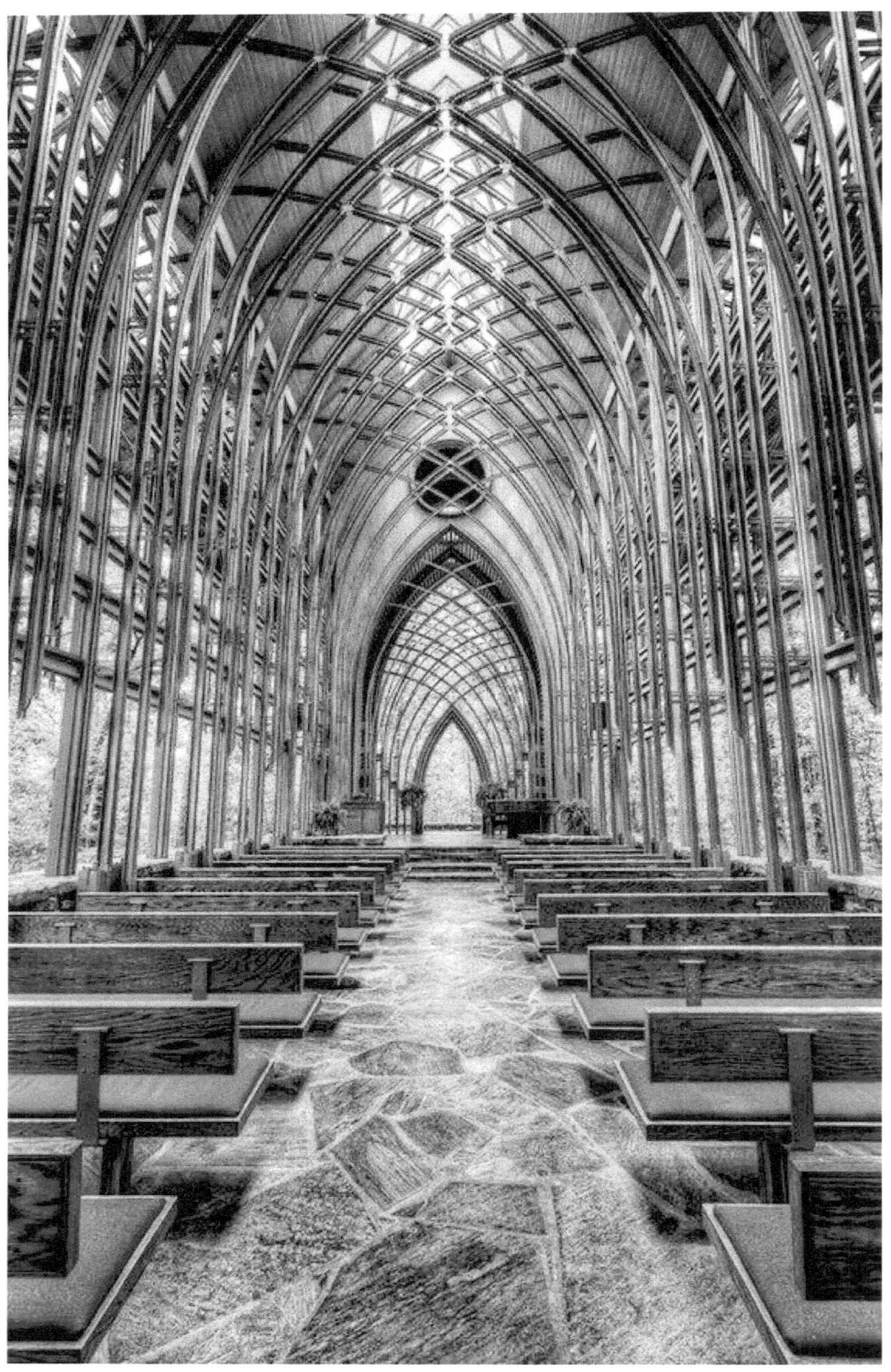

Chapter 15
Benefits From Entering the Akasha

*I*n my many years of accessing the Akasha I was either quickly or eventually led to several benefits from using the Records and therein found even more unique pathways into knowing myself at deeper levels.

Accessing the Records and looking into your own Book of Life is enough by itself to keep you engaged in personal study for the rest of this earthly lifetime. Coming in contact with your past incarnations and studying those personalities is quite a body of work spiritually once you realize the magnitude of it all.

All of the karmas from those lifetimes, whether good, bad or indifferent and the many hats we've worn including all of the things we've experienced and learned in those past lives. All of the trades and crafts we've learned, all of the relationships we've had with families, friends and lovers and many other aspects. As you get into investigating the deeper levels that make you who you are, there are many intricacies that you will find and may show up in your current life circumstances, relationships, and personality traits.

At this point you can see there's quite a lot of personal growth study that can come through to you. The interesting thing in addition to it all, is that it's been there waiting for you the whole time. Just for you, personally, until such time that you might be ready or find your way into the Records. And that's why I am here with you working on all of this.

No one in this world or beyond has any power over keeping you from the Akashic Records or Your Book of Life within the Akashic Records. For the most part it's been lost over time. Whether naturally forgotten, esoterically hidden, or purposefully buried, the song remains the same.

Here we are in a future time of the ancients when we come to realize the power of our own Soul and to find ways to connect with it's knowledge, wisdom and memories through the Records. Now in this lifetime you have the opportunity to go into your own Soul which is always and has always been connected to your Soul Records in heaven. That in and of itself is an amazing gift to have access to.

Many of us who have found the Records have

reported deeper levels of personal activity and additional benefits to be gained from practicing in this art. In my learning and experiencing with the Akasha I have found many unique benefits that can be gained just by accessing. We'll bring those to the light in this chapter. I will say though, that in order to start achieving the best and most natural benefit from your practice it is better to just focus on naturally learning to read the Records first and then going to the next level.

So let's talk about these 'other' unique side effects of developing a practice of connecting to your Soul's Records. This is the profound ground breaking dynamic that is being shared here in this material for the first time anywhere: The Stream of the Soul that connects into the Records has Divine hidden capabilities within it's natural essence.

As you continue to access the Akashic Records and more specifically your own Book of Life, you start to build a continually strengthening cord into your own Records. This cord or stream is your Divine Soul energy moving between the Soul body and the Soul Records. This has the power to bring more vital essence into your body and energy fields. This has the power to heal things in your body, mind and spirit. This has the power to clear and heal your karma and also to clear Soul contracts. What I call **Akashic Shamanic** work that I have developed and can be experienced. The

Soul stream can also bring back Soul fragments as your guides and the masters and Keepers of the Records are involved.

The implications of this are huge. So now for the first time since ancient times you are getting the inside information. Remember this as you move forward. It will be more beneficial for you to focus on your own natural Akashic reading first. What I'm stating here is parallel to what the masters knew about the **siddhis** or special powers that were gained by practicing advanced yogic techniques.

Manifesting thought to form, bi-location, extended astral projection, becoming super small or large, or becoming invisible are just some of these ancient powers. Often the students would think glamorously about these powers and what they might do with them and in so doing they would miss or forget the true focus of the spiritual studies and path.

In the same way, the special powers are but by-products of a deeper study. Don't let these unique gifts be your only focus. Continue focusing on primary access of the Akashic Records while knowing that there are other natural gifts that will come in as an offshoot of being on the spiritual path. We will take this dynamic to the next level in Vol. 3.

The Akasha or 'sky library' has the nature and element of air. So as you practice naturally over time you may find a very clear soft air-like quality to reading of the Records. You will also be accessing higher dimensions so it will have a continual unique effect with your body, mind and spirit over time.

Hold sacred these gifts that you will receive through practicing. Be reverent and kind in your approach with the Akashic Records and the higher beings who work there. It's not just a public library to be taken for granted and used for any purpose. This is God's library of all the Earth Souls so be good, kind and responsible when you're in the presence of the Records.

Other benefits include becoming more intuitive and becoming more psychic. As you access your Soul field through accessing the stream, you'll will be able to use what is called **intuition**. This is the 'psychic' nature of energy coming from your Soul. If you get quiet and really listen, your Soul has unique messages on everything.

Your Soul is the one part of the human system that we usually don't hear or feel energetically most of the time because it's so high in vibration. We can feel psychic energy or mind energy. We can feel within the body. We can feel or sense from within the chakras and we can also feel energy from outside sources. Different forms of healing energy projected from other people. The hardest thing for us to feel is our Soul energy because it's so quiet. This may be for the most part why the Soul information was lost over time and then through organized religion we were told we only get one life and then the Soul either goes to heaven or hell. As you continue to practice your Akashic Records abilities you will notice that you will become more aware of the Soul's energy and it's intuition.

This information on the Akashic Records and connecting to your Book of Life will naturally and gradually put you directly in contact with your Soul. As you continue to access the Records, the upload and download streams are happening simultaneously. This stream composed of Divine Intelligence fortifies your Soul.

As this happens your Soul becomes more naturally connected with the physical body, the chakras, the mind and the senses. Over time you will start to feel the presence of the Soul. Your True Self. There aren't many other studies that I know of to put you directly back in touch with your True Celestial Soul. Working with the Akashic Records will definitely do that while fortifying your Soul and all other parts of your being at the same time.

As you continually access the Records you will naturally continue to become more psychic. Over the course of my experiences I've witnessed many brilliant psychics. Many of them would come to my classes to learn more about the Records and the deeper levels of intuition that are available. Often people may think, and I certainly did upon first starting, that maybe we're not psychic enough. In truth, everyone is, we just need to tune into it and

BENEFITS FROM ENTERING THE AKASHA

turn it on.

I remember thinking: 'What do I have to offer? What, if anything, do I have to share?' I never practiced becoming psychic, I just practiced reading the Records and it helped me to become more naturally psychic as an extra added benefit.

There are some great naturally gifted psychics out there. I never considered myself to be one of them. But as I continued reading the Records, my natural psychic abilities started to come more and more online. So as I read the Records now it is a natural blend of psychic (mind field) and intuitive (soul field) awareness that gives me a full scope or spectrum when working with others. I have also found that after a while I could shift between the mind and Soul seamlessly as needed. Did I have anything to offer? I'll let all the people that I've given sessions to speak for me on that. They have given me such detailed confirmations over the years that I find it truly a blessing that the Keepers of the Akashic Records found me.

Yes you will become more psychic also as a result. Now if you're already psychic, it will not only teach you to view or see in different ways, it may also speak to you in new ways. Sometimes it has a way of undoing what you're doing with your reading style and bring you all sorts of new information. The one thing that it will definitely undo is your ego. After meeting many gifted psychics, I discovered one thing that many readers have had in common was that the ego was in the driver's seat.

Now I'm not saying they were ego maniacs or wrong in any way. It's the nature of the psyche and personality to be accessing mental waves and trying to interpret these through the scope of the mind, personality and the communication skills. As this happens the ego chimes in and the ego loves to manage things even in psychic readings. When you access the Akashic you are moving through your Soul where the ego doesn't exist so you will get a whole new spectrum of messages. Maybe you even get some of the same messages but now they come through in a different style or story through the higher mind. It is a good idea to always ask yourself: 'On what level am I getting this information?' Ask Spirit, God or your guides to humbly interpret the messages as they come through with gratitude for receiving.

There a many benefits that you can receive from reading the Akashic Records. They are within you and waiting to develop and unfold as you steadily continue developing your skills.

Keep up the good (God) work!

Benefits from Entering the Akasha

Chapter 16
Releasing Emotional Pain & Fear

Suffering from emotional pain or fear can be some of the most traumatic things to experience. As a child we may have had reprimands that the psyche now deems as stressful in the memory of it all. So many people have suffered physical, mental, emotional and even sexual abuse that the numbers are astonishing. Many people are carrying the burdens of these old wounds in their bodies, minds and spirits. The body tissue has the memory of these events even down to a cellular level as does the body spirit, the astral, mental and emotional bodies and sometimes the Soul.

Could you imagine a society with more happy, healthy people completely free of any past traumas? It would definitely give us a foot up in the evolution of humanity. No matter what the case is for individuals in today's world we have so many new practices, healing techniques and therapies that it truly is a gift to be able to utilize whatever can help us all to move forward in our lives.

No matter what a person has been through at any stage of their life, we as humans have a tendency to stuff things down deep inside in order to keep going. It's a survival mechanism that we use in order to keep going in life. A survival tactic you might say. Another way of looking at it is that we put layers around us or put on a shield of armour to hide behind so that no one can see our weakness and often we can't feel it either.

Emotional pain and fear can cause physical health issues as the body of a person tries to balance the situation from within it's tissue. The body is very responsive to it's surroundings as well as emotional and mental conditioning. Anything from a sore throat to advanced forms of dis-ease can take place in the body.

The best strategy is to start going within through meditation and taking a good look at life and start to change and release anything that can be released for all around total health and well being.

Sometimes when we start the process we may have reactions in the body as old energies of traumas are released. The body may be anxious, tight or tense until we revisit into some old wounds from the past and let them come to the surface. As this happens the ego, the subconscious and sometimes the immune system as well as the whole body could have a reaction in order to maintain balance. If it were any small thing we wouldn't be having a reaction to the healing or self introspection. If you go into an old tragedy or lifetime wound and you feel no charge of energy around it, then you are done with it and whatever it was meant to show you or teach you is done.

Be gentle with yourself above all else. Releasing all judgements can help you find the thread to your healing much quicker. Sometimes your body needs some love and needs to know that you have good intentions in it's favor instead of just pushing it forward. Nothing is more important than your personal well being. So make the best of everything and always do your best to shine your Light in the world.

Fear can also be debilitating. It interrupts our free flow of energy. If fear is running in the back ground of a person's life movie it can have the affect of holding them back or even to stopping them dead in their tracks. It can keep a person from healing and it can keep a person in lack unable to move forward towards success.

Fear and anger are closely related and anger can be debilitating as well. The ego will utilize both fear and anger as survival mechanisms in it's fight to maintain a certain balance or level within a person's life which can also be limiting. The ego will continue to run the show until it is put on standby. Working with the Soul is the perfect way to do this. When the Soul starts to take over the healing process the ego will stand down. It may take a bit of coercion in order to be persuaded, but usually it will listen if your approach is steady. The Soul can and will sooner or eventually override the ego.

The main challenge that we all have with releasing unwanted energy or memories trapped in the tissue is based around the sentient feelings of them. When we open up a personal issue for healing, we feel the remembrance of that event. Feelings of fear, anger, resentment and any other uncomfortable emotions, even nausea or pain in the body may come up to the surface to be experienced.

As these things come up, the main thing that we experience is the tension, stress or discomfort of it all. Here's the boon: When issues, memories or emotions come up they are trying to R E L E A S E from the Self. *BUT* the ego often grabs a hold of the energy of the whole dynamic and tries to pull it back in. The ego is attempting to stuff it back down and hide it away. The trick is to remain PRESENT to any thing of this nature and breathing through it and focusing on RELEASING IT. It can be done! Because the ego is involved on a base level, it may feel like it's so close to the project that it tries to delegate the manage all things.

The Higher Self and the Soul know other wise. They have the upper hand and can intervene and even involve the spirit guides and the healers on the other side to help you move through it all more easily.

This is important in relation to our Akashic Records studies. As you get into your studies maybe some things from past events have been part of your reason for getting into this work. If so you are in a powerful place for change. In studying this material to learn the dynamics of it all, you may find that upon getting into the work, you will be guided through certain things naturally that could bring up memories that you can heal and clear.

You may also uncover deeper levels of things that have been with you from other lifetimes. Another magical point: Sometimes when you have tried everything else in your healing tool kit and nothing is working, you must go to the Soul and the past lives in order to find the cause of current maladies, limitations or suffering.

The Soul is connected to all lifetimes of a person simultaneously although your reference will be on the current body, senses and life movie. Beyond the constructs of linear time is continual in the Eternal Now moment. The Soul operates in this realm as does everyone and everything else outside of the 3rd dimension.

So as discussed in the last chapter the stream of energy running between the Akasha and the Soul field has abilities and benefits to strengthen and grow it's own connection, and to enhance the Soul field. As this happens the connections from a person's Soul field go out to the past and other lifetimes or realities and are communicated with energetically as well.

The natural dynamic of the Soul is to heal and balance all lifetimes, especially if you're working in the Records in this lifetime. The energy will stream from the Soul to balance or heal things going on in other time lines. As this happens your current reality may be affected by these dynamics as an extra added benefit or gift from doing the work.

This often happens to people naturally sometimes who are doing everything right and have really focused on success and healing and even growing their spiritual connection. If you're doing everything to heal that you can and are still not able to get ahead or break some sort of invisible chain, then I urge you to look into the Records or to seek the aid of a good Akashic Reader and see what's going on at your Soul level. Something(s) may be pulling at your Soul's energy in another time line such as a traumatic event, an illness, or a conflict of some sort with others that your Soul is sending energy to.

I have often had people come to me for just these reasons. Sometimes they even know something is off in another time line. They can sense it, and may not have any intuitive information about it or if they do they're not quite sure how to go about fixing, healing or clearing the situation. I use special techniques for this in my session work that I will be sharing in the advanced workshops. If you feel that you need help along these lines then say a prayer asking for help and look for a right source of healing. When you ask on this level rest assured your guides are already working on it! These are some of the inner workings and dynamics of the Soul and the Akashic Records that once you learn about through experience you are advancing your own Self Knowing process which is why we're all here in the first place. To Know the Self collectively and individually.

Divine Blessings to You on Your Soul's Journey.

As you look into your life with no conflict you release it and embrace it simultaneously. This is where the healing occurs naturally, just be present.

Journey Exercise 6

INNER CHILD LIFETIME EMOTIONAL HEALING

*Read the Script
and then practice your self guided visualization.*

This is a guided meditation for healing your inner child and your life experiences. As you read through these pages, you can then settle yourself and become ready to have your own healing experience. Please get comfortable and start to relax finding a place to sit, recline or lay down. If you are laying down a light blanket to cover the body can be very helpful. And a pillow under the knees.

I recommend having a glass of water within reach. As you start to get comfortable start to take some long slow deep breaths and close your eyes. Just continue to breathe in and out long and slow. As you continue to relax down your whole body becomes loose and limp and lazy. And as you relax now your toes, ankles and feet. Relaxing now your shins and calves, and your knees. Relaxing the space behind the knees. Relaxing your thighs and hamstrings. Your hips, waist and pelvis are all completely relaxed. As you relax down, down even deeper, breathing long slow and relaxed breaths. Your lower stomach and lower back are all completely relaxed as the relaxing energy now moves up your spine to soothe your whole back. As you continue to relax your torso and chest all completely relaxed. Make sure your shoulders are dropped and relaxed.

Relaxing now your neck as you relax down, down, down even deeper. Releasing all the concerns of the day and the world, Relax your head and your eyes. Relax your face, and your cheeks, your ears are completely relaxed. Continuing to relax deeper and releasing all stress.

As you continue to relax, become aware of your whole being. Your Body, Mind, Heart and Spirit. See now a beautiful emerald green light in your heart. As you breathe in and out it pulses with energy. Becoming brighter and deeper with a great gentle soothing light. As you look into this light you see now the trees in a beautiful outdoor setting. The trees, the sky, the clouds and the green grass. See yourself there now as a little boy or girl. See yourself playing on the grass, running, walking, riding your bike. What do you want to do here as the little child? Take some time to be here for a few moments.

As the sun starts to move into late afternoon, you hear a voice calling you home. Calling you back to your house. So as you gather any toys or bicycle you ride back home. Going into the house you come into your room where you find yourself there as your Future Self, your now current adult self. You know that it is You though you have grown. Walking over to your adult self you touch your shoulder and as soon as you do this your consciousness moves back into your current self. As you now relax you see your little one, your Inner Child Self looking at you as they touch your left shoulder. They are smiling at You, glad to be here with You. This is You looking at You, You connecting with You.

You now see a very soft golden white glow coming from above as a portal opens and coming down through the portal, the great Arc Angels come to form a ring around you and your inner child. Arc Angels Metatron and Michael, Gabriel and Raphael. Jophiel and Sandalphon, Chamuel and Ariel, Uriel, Daniel, Haniel, Zadkiel and many more.

As they stand around you as great pillars of Light. You and your child self start to become very bright light. Feeling light as a feather now as you start to float up through the ceiling. The Arc Angels are floating with you as they bring you up through the beam of light. Through the portal the Light engulfs you as you float up through the sky. You now see the heavenly celestial bodies of stars as you float up through the atmosphere. Continuing up, up and away with the Arc Angels around you in a great circle, you now move into the clouds as the bright white of the clouds cover everything in pure white.

As you come out of the clouds you find yourself atop a sea of clouds and standing now before a great temple. With You here are your Child Self and the Arc Angels. As a pair of great ancient doors before you slowly begin to open they reveal the inside of the great temple of the Akashic Hall of Records. There is a great gathering of friends waiting for you here.

The Keepers of the Records and many masters have awaited this visit. Jesus and Mary Magdalene are here. Also Mother Mary is here and they all smile and welcome you. Quan Yin and the Bodhisattvas are here. Serapis Bey pats your shoulder as Kuthumi and El Morya embrace you. Buddha now greets you with a healing mudra as a blessing. St Germain drapes a purple cloak around your shoulders. Babaji floats in and joins the group as his gentle divine vibration and voice give another blessing here to You and everyone.

All of the Arc Angels stand around everyone towering and talking, enjoying this great gathering. Merlin now appears and comes up behind your Child Self. Holding a staff in one hand he touches your child's shoulder. As he raises his staff to now open another portal through the ceiling of the Great Hall. The stars of the constellations are now exposed in the sky above.

The Keeper of the Records summons your attention as you turn to join him. You are now facing your Book of Life. And as Merlin calls down a star from the night sky it floats down gently and into the room and hovers over the Great Book of Life. As the star expands it creates a crystal sphere.

As you now look into the great sphere, you see a life event that is in need of healing. So as you view this life event from the Akashic Sphere, study it here and see and feel what is happening in that moment, and as you look into it notice all of the compassion that you have in your heart for you in that moment of time. Feel the love and compassion of all of the Masters as they lift you up. There is no judgement only Love.

And as you're sending healing loving energy to that part of yourself in that time, you realize now how you made it through those times. You were right here with yourself as a Divine Guide along with all of the Masters and Angels holding space for dear sweet beautiful You.

As you continue now, go to yet another and another time in your life where you can receive healing from your Self here in the Akasha with the Masters and Angels. The great lovers of life and humanity. As you continue take as much time as you need to be thorough so that you can come to a sense of completion with everything that you've been through and everything that you need to view in the Spheres. As you view your life events through the Divine energy of the Akasha they are naturally healed in the presence of the Divine Masters.

As you look into your life with no conflict you release it and embrace it simultaneously. This is where the healing occurs naturally, just be present.

As you have now taken ample time to view so many things in your life that needed healing and compassion, here you are now back in the Great Hall. As you look over Mother Mary is picking up your Little One as she rocks them gently. And now you notice several other versions of yourself here with the group. It's You from times in your life that you've looked into. Your 10-12 yr. Self, Your teenager Self, Your young adult self. The Selves that went through any accidents or illnesses, they are all here too.

And now you see your family members joining the group. All having such a wonderful time with the Masters and Angels. As Christ now comes before You, he places both hands on your shoulders and he sends his powerful healing energy into your Soul. He knows what you've been through and it's now time to release the burdens of the past and to Live and Love in the Eternal Now moment from Now on. You are Blessed, You are Healed.

All of your other Selves and your Little One join around you as they now step into you with grace and ease. As you now pick up and hold your Inner Child.

Welcome Home. And with that said the Angels now return you to your room safely down through the portal as you gently rest now. Come back to the moment and take some to realize and to process the healing that you have just received. Be gentle with yourself. You may want to journal about your experience.

Living life and experiencing from this moment forth with all of the Peace, Love and Blessings that are Yours. Amen.

Chapter 17
Journey Home to the Eternal Moment

This will be a guided activation that you will receive

We have come far Dear Soul, all the way across the Universe from the First Moment of Creator. Travelling through the stars and visiting other distant planets and civilizations. You have come so far and yet the journey is not over. In some ways it is just beginning.

Through the far reaches of the galaxy you found home here. And you found members of your Soul group. You found family and you started to remember to learn how to feel and to love in this sentient world. You remembered how to be creative and you shared it with others and with the world.

You dreamed of a life of helping others, enjoying life and learning how to feel. You beamed down from the Akashic Records once again as you found the right mother and father to continue your creative expressions of learning, loving, living and creating.

So many times you came down and graced the world with your presence. So many other Souls you have loved here and far beyond in the ever after and in distant reaches of the Universe.

You are Divine and You are Love. You are all that you'd hoped you'd be and more. You've never given up and always moved forward to continue the Soul's mission of evolution.

Through your many visits here you have met, interacted and befriended many Souls. There were even some that could not understand your Light. They needed to dance with You in order to be lifted into the Light of their own Soul.

The Divine interaction between Souls or Soul mates as we call it here. Those who have crossed paths before in other lifetimes. Those who can touch the Light of another Soul and bring that essence into their own world. With the Truth of all Souls being of the pure essence and part of Creator. All Souls unique and unequalled in their own expression. As they fly, dance, sing and journey across the stars migrating through space and time.

As the Souls fill up the bodies of beings of every creed and race, we express our greatness. We enter that place within realities where we can make choices and experience the magic of the world around us.

As all the Souls of Creator throughout creation itself move and breathe together in unison and uniquely apart from one another. We experience the oneness through communion and the individuality through our personal life movie.

Our life spans are varied throughout different civilizations. Our time is Now. In the Eternal Now Moment always and beyond the limits of linear time. This dream, this life is seemingly not long enough as the moments disappear behind us in this 3 dimensional reality. As the generations change and all that is now will be lost or remembered in memories of the heart and mind. Yet the great Heart and Mind of Universal Intelligence have not forgotten you or any other Soul in any way. The Great Heart and Mind speaks to You through the Eternal Now Moment. Always present as an Eternal Light lifting You up to recognize You as part of itself.

As you now close your eyes and go into your heart space connecting with the great heart space of Divine Intelligence. You are now being transported into the great Hall of Akashic Wisdom. The Divine Light of the Hall of Records is shining through your Soul. As you see the rooms full of books and scrolls. A very soft and sweet feeling resides here. This is your library, your study. The Library of Souls. As you now see your personal book open here in front of you. It is time to know yourself. It is time to come home. To read the many stories that you wrote. To look into other worlds and other lives and to see and feel the great life missions you have been on.

As you look into the Book of Life there is a great white candle standing before you now on this table by the Book. This great candle has a flame that never flickers. Always steady and always burning. This Eternal Flame has the essence and quality of Infinity. As you look into the flame you are blessed with the release of any and all unrest or sadness. All pain and fear dissipates in the presence of this Holy Flame. Ever burning, ever loving broadcasting a signal out across the Universes that will remain a still beacon for all Souls. This flame will be the call to your heart and the signal to call you back to yourself. As you recognize your own Self, and all of the Love that you are, through the Grace that brings us here.

As you look into the Eternal Flame of Holy Light the light of the flame gives birth to a second flame, a twin flame. The floating flame moves away from the candle. As it hovers in front of you like a gentle fairy. A Great Gift is being given to you as the flame now moves closer to you. As you feel the light now moving closer to your body, this hovering holy flame moves directly into your chest, into your heart.

This Light knows how to guide you. This Light knows how to heal you. Always together with you this Holy Flame keeps you safe and lets you know that you are never alone, always with us and always provided for. It will always be with you forever and a day. This Light will speak to others through your heart and show them their own Light. Your heart will soon light up the world. Everyday and in every way you get one step closer to touching another Soul. Doing the Great Work as they call you forth in the Light to be their messenger. To bring all of the Soul pieces of Creator back together as one song, one uni-verse. Every smile, every good intention, every helping hand brings the world one step closer to realizing the we are all the Light and we are having a magical miracle movie experience here together.

The Light knows how to find it's own. The Eternal Light knows the love and grace of your heart and it has come home. It has found it's destiny. To be inside your Heart, inside your Soul as a beacon shining to all other Souls. This is your destiny and this is your gift to go forth as a Soul with a great Light that is shinning with all other Souls. And now you have come home within yourself. Together forever with the One Love that is You.

God Bless You, I Love You, Amen.

Exercise 7

THE COSMIC EXPANSION PROCESS
A GALACTIVATION

© Copyright Bill Foss 2019 All Rights Reserved
Visualization Meditation Integrative Process
*Read the Script
and then practice your self guided visualization meditation.*

This is a guided meditation visualization process which has many integrative benefits. We will cover the benefits step by step as we go over the process together.

As the ancient Siddhas of India and their study of the ancient natural sciences has revealed profound levels of knowledge, wisdom and information sometimes unparalleled by modern science. This process is from these ancient times and has roots back to even earlier times within Atlantis and Lemuria. This is a guided meditation process that was brought to me through deep meditation as I sat quietly and practiced the long version of the Gayatri mantra. The long version of the Gayatri mantra activates the chakras along the spine and awakens them with the earth energy in a wonderful and effective way.

As I continued to practice I was shown connections through the crown charka to the sun. When I channelled this it was no surprise and more of a synchronicity with the progressive creative process of ancient information coming through in conjunction with practicing the ancient art of Solar Gazing.

So as we start the Cosmic Expansion process. Get comfortable sitting in an up-right position with your feet on the floor and your spine straight. Your hands relaxed in your lap or on your knees. You may want to use the Earth Mudra which is touching the tip of the 3rd or ring finger to the tip of your thumb. Do this with both hands. Some mudra practitioners believe that lifting the hands slightly away from the legs and opening the spaces under the arms is beneficial for increased energy flow. I recommend experimenting over the coarse of several practices to see what works best for you. You may use these subtly different variations from time to time. The main key is to be relaxed.

For those of us who want to supercharge this energy visualization process, I recommend learning the long version of the Earth Mantra and use it spoken aloud, chanted or sung, and other times even pronounced silently in the mind. Some schools of thought suggest that a whisper can be stronger than a full vocal pronunciation, while using silent mantras can produce sensitively different energy effects. Try learning and speaking it aloud first to familiar yourself with the tones and the way they influence and work with the energy in your body. This mantra will open, balance and align your energy first with the true vibration of the Earth and her energies.

The Gayatri Mantra (long version):
Om Bhur Om Bhavaha Om Swaha Om Maha
Om Janaha Om Tapaha Om Satyam
Om Tat Savitur Varenyam Bhargo Devasya Dhimahi
Dhiyo Yonaha Prachodayat

Sounded out pronunciation:
Om Boor Om Boovaha Om Swaha Om Maha
Om Jon Aha Om Top Aha Om Sat Yam ...
Om Tot Sava Tour Var In Yam Bargo Deva See Ya Dee Ma Hee Dee Yo yo Naha Pra Cho Day Ot

Another powerful vocalization for working with any mantra will be to chant the mantra at least 4 times in a strong and mono tone voice or as close as possible. In eastern traditions it is known that it only takes 4 repetitions of any mantra to activate the energy of that mantra. Classic mantra practice involves chanting 108 repetitions of each mantra with a mala. (traditional prayer beads)

The syllables are composed of Sanskrit language, an ancient dialect used by spiritual civilizations of the East. When the syllables are used in this way, they bring vibrations into certain parts of the body, the head, the energy fields and the chakras. The long version of the Gayatri mantra specifically charges and opens the chakras along the spine including the 3rd eye brow center and the crown chakra center.

The Cosmic Expansion Process is as follows:

As you connect your base chakra with the energy at the center of the earth, see the lower end of the spine at tailbone area and pelvis, and visualize a stream of energy coming from the center of the earth straight up to the base of the spine and then continuing up through the spine. Activating the chakras and the spinal fluid.

As the energy continues to rise up through the Base center, then second chakra, solar plexus, heart chakra, throat chakra, third eye (brow center) and pineal gland (in the center of the brain) and on up to the crown. See the energy continuing straight up from your crown and into the center of the sun. So you are aligning your axis points between the center of the Earth and your base chakra and the crown chakra and the center of the Sun.

Now as you hold that visualization. See now your energy fields coming out from around your body expanding to cover the whole earth. Continuing to expand now even farther out to include all of the planets of the solar system.

The Earth is your home and as you practice this

visualization, connect to this local solar system which is your neighborhood. As you expand your energy fields out in a great sphere to include all the orbiting planets, you are merging your energy with these celestial bodies. A hidden key here for you is this: When you *merge* your energy with the planets you transcend their planetary astrological properties. As they answer your connection with them there is no longer a push/pull effect coming directly from these planets. That said the positive attributes of the planets in relation to you, your everyday life and life path will still be intact and help you continue creating in a good way.

Now let's take the visualization a step farther and move through the Center of the Sun and all the way back to Creator God of Love at the Great Central Sun. Feel the Divine Energy. The Love, the Peace, the Creativity, the Healing Perfection.

The idea with this process is that you are working with energy of your Soul, your Mind, your energy fields and your Consciousness in new multi-faceted and multi-dimensional way. This is different than astral projection in that we are not just floating out of body aimlessly to see what we can find in space. We are working with our local cosmic neighborhood and we are purposefully using spheres and the axis point straight line connections of the earth and sun with the body.

Now as you continue all the visualization focal

points, let's add to all this the idea, movement or even centrifugal feeling that as you're expanding in multiple directions and ways. The Earth is moving in orbit around the sun at 66,000 miles per hour! The other planets are all moving at varied speeds and our local Sun is moving at 52,000 miles per hour through space. This may add to the feeling of the Cosmic Expansion process. You may experience an instantaneous feeling of flying or expansion. Additionally if you are living on the surface of planet Earth you are rotating with the surface on Earth's axis at 1,040 miles per hour.

You are expanding the fields in ways that the mind has to sometimes catch up with. Your mind will hold for you the visions of base and crown chakras connected with the centers of the earth and sun. Your mind will hold for you seeing and experiencing your energy fields expanding out to include the whole solar system. And your mind will also hold for you the expansion through the sun to the Great Central Sun. All of this happening simultaneously.

Upon starting to practice this technique your mind will move around from place to place. This is natural as you're getting a feel and practicing visualization and expansion at the same time. As you continue to practice this, your mind and ego will give up in ways and also expand out with the rest of your fields including your Soul field. The Cosmic Expansion process has multiple benefits which I will list some of

Cosmic Expansion Process

here and let you find the rest on your own:

Continued practice of the Cosmic Expansion Process will help to positively integrate astrological effects of the zodiac and the planets they are associated with.

As you practice expanding you are exercising the Soul field which is beneficial on many levels for your conscious recognition of it. You will be benefiting directly from the organic solar energy, earth energy and energy of the starlight traveling through space to reach us here.

As the energy travels up from the center of the earth and through your chakras along the spine and up and out the crown to connect with the sun, you are chanting the long version of the Gayatri mantra at least 4 times. This activates the chakras between the earth and sun. If you do this process without the mantra you will be just fine, and for some of us it may even work more easily.

This process is helpful to supersede any negative or varied energies, social movements, clearing on all levels, and aligning yourself with a more creative and joyful existence including relationships, health and prosperity.

I'm including here the short version of the Gayatri mantra. The short version for most yogic practitioners is the most recognizable and used more often in Kirtan singing meditation gatherings. The long version is what we will be utilizing in the

Cosmic Expansion process. You will be able to tell a noticeable difference between the long version and short version of the Gayatri (Earth) mantra.

The Gayatri Mantra Short version:
Om Bhur Bhuva Swaha,
Tat Savitur Varenyam,
Bhargo Devasya Dhimahi
Dhiyo Yonaha Prachodayat
Sounded out and pronounced:

Om Boor Boova Swaha
Tot Sav uh Tour Var In Yam
Bargo Deva See Ya Dee Ma Hee
Dee Yoyo Naha Pra Cho Day Ot

PLANETARY REVOLUTION

0. Our local Sun is moving through space at 52,000 miles per hour.
1. Mercury is the fastest planet, which speeds around the sun at 107,082 miles per hour.
2. Venus is the second fastest planet with an orbital speed of 78,337 miles per hour.
3. Earth, our home planet of Earth speeds around the sun at a rate of 66,615 miles per hour.
4. Mars, with an orbital speed of 53,858 miles per hour
5. Jupiter travels at an orbital speed of 29,236 miles per hour.
6. Saturn travels at 9.69 km/s, or 21,675 miles per

hour.
7. Uranus has an orbital speed of 15,233 miles per hour.
8. Neptune travels around the sun at 12,146 miles per hour.
9. Pluto takes 248 years to orbit the sun and travels at 18,000 miles per hour.

KEPLER'S FIRST LAW DESCRIBES THE SHAPE OF AN ORBIT

The orbit of a planet around the Sun (or of a satellite around a planet) is not a perfect circle. It is an ellipse or a "flattened" circle. The Sun (or the center of the planet) occupies one focus of the ellipse. A focus is one of the two internal points that help determine the shape of an ellipse. The distance from one focus to any point on the ellipse and then back to the second focus is always the same.

KEPLER'S SECOND LAW DESCRIBES THE WAY AN OBJECT'S SPEED VARIES ALONG ITS ORBIT

A planet's orbital speed changes, depending on how far it is from the Sun. The closer a planet is to the Sun, the stronger the Sun's gravitational pull on it, and the faster the planet moves. The farther it is from the Sun, the weaker the Sun's gravitational pull, and the slower it moves in its orbit.

KEPLER'S THIRD LAW COMPARES THE MOTION OF OBJECTS IN ORBITS OF DIFFERENT SIZES

A planet farther from the Sun not only has a longer path than a closer planet, but it also travels slower, since the Sun's gravitational pull on it is weaker. Therefore, the larger a planet's orbit, the longer the planet takes to complete it.

Teaching Terms
for the Akashic Records Center Certification Process

Akashic Vision Journey Experience - The energetic experience of having your inner vision come on through your eyes and your third eye. Seeing in 3D lucid inner vision which can be momentary or continually streaming. This can be either animated movies or stationary pictures, images, colors or words and/or symbols.

Akashic Light Symbols - A higher dimensional harmonic language of light symbols that are specific to the Akashic Records in frequency. The original symbol language that all Earth/planetary languages and dialects come from. It is possible to read and to translate this language through meditation, visions and writing in order to receive direct messages from the Akasha.

Akashic Shamanic - A form of inquiry and Soul Healing developed by Bill Foss which employs the dynamics of both the Akashic and Shamanic. Akashic being higher dimensional sky based energy and Shamanic being deep Earth based energy.

Book of Life - Within the Akashic Records each

Soul has it's own collection of thought, word and deed. Responses and reactions from every lifetime that it has experienced while incarnated in human form. The Book of Life is used by the Soul, and God to guide each individual Soul's purpose, experiences and evolution.

Body Spirit - The part of a person's Soul that more deeply inhabits the physical body, it's organs and it's systems. This part of the Soul carries all of the cellular memories from the current and past lifetimes.

Celestial Soul - This part of the Soul comes from the stars. It can be directly linked to Creator God, the Great Central Sun, or other incarnations in civilizations among the stars prior to earthly incarnations. This part of the Soul carries Divine Intelligence to heal and to connect with it's origins and other Soul family members.

Creative Affirmation Thought Commands Primarily used for programming and reprogramming the conscious and the subconscious minds. These are comprised of words, mantras, prayers, affirmations and declarations to the Universe, the external world, and to the self to bring the self into alignment with that which one desires to have in their life experience.

Creative Entanglement - The connections of a person's Soul to all of the lifetimes. And the connection from the human body to the Soul and into the Records which utilizes the principles of quantum energy as well as past, present, future.

Divine Timing - Also known as Serendipity or

Teaching Terms

Synchronicity. Those times when the Universe and the teachers, angels, guides and healers working with you on the other side bring into your time and space the perfect timing for protection, healing, manifesting something for you, or meeting a certain individual which you are destined to meet. Often Grace is involved in these situations.

Divine Right - Also known as a person's birthright. Knowledge and Wisdom that would be freely given for you and the ability to experience: Joy, Love, Spirituality, Access to your Book of Life, etc.

Divine Universal Law of Free Will - In alignment with your Divine Right, This Universal Law states that no one or no thing has power over you unless you agree or consent to it whether knowingly or unknowingly. Often this happens unknowingly which then does allow for Divine Intervention from another person, spirit, angels, guides or God to remove unwanted interference.

Etheric Wheel of Lifetimes - This is the incarnation cycle and the collection of all of a soul's lifetimes. Often illustrated as a wheel with spokes or connections from each lifetime on the wheel to the Soul as the central hub to all incarnations of lifetimes.

Eternal Now Moment - The continual streaming of present awareness. The continual series of unfolding moments. When you realize that continually you are stepping beyond linear time and space and in direct alignment with Universal Intelligence. Continual focus on the present. *Example: All past, present and future moments exist within the Eternal Now.*

Higher Self - The part of a person's being that is working in the other or higher dimensions. Also known as the Light Body or Angelic Self. Usually depicted by a luminous figure over the physical body.

Inner Child - Each of us has the remembrances of our childhood. As we connect back to this part of ourselves we relive or re-experience emotions, thought patterns and situations. We integrate the Inner Child for the purposes of self healing, release and empowerment in our current life.

Knowing Way of Truth and Light - The original Spiritual light teachings from Atlantis. Also carried forward by Thoth the Atlantean from those times into Egyptian times. Also referred to by Jesus the Christ as the Knowing Way of Truth and Light, the Knowing Way or simply the Way.

Quantum Time Line Healing - A healing modality developed by Bill Foss which involves healing of the ancestors, the bloodline and the family tree of an individual. QTLH involves travelling backwards and forwards along the time line simultaneously in order to pin point moments of injury or trauma.

Past, Present & Future Selves - The child self or inner child, the present day self and the higher of perfect God self. Also correlated to the Subconscious, Conscious and Super conscious minds.

Shamanic Soul Retrieval - The process of healing used by a shaman or shamanic practitioner to bring back lost pieces of a persons Soul energy. Often when Soul energy is missing, taken or becomes lost, a person may operate at a deficit or uneasiness until the missing Soul fragments are returned. Shamanism is an ancient tribal practice of working with the earth's energy and the animal familiars to bring back a person's energy to them and to release anything that has been with them whether elemental energy, another person's energy or a non-physical being which has attached to them for some reason or another.

Soul Timing - This is what is discoverable through studying your Book of Life. Time is overlapping in places and not only a series of linear events. Our Soul has scheduled events to experience which can be altered through spiritual development. Soul Timing is also associated with Divine Timing.

Streaming Akashic Vision - This occurs when you are fully engaged in your visual Akashic Records practice and there is a direct connection between the Records and your Soul energy streaming down into your mind's eye, your senses, your physical and energy bodies and your chakras. It becomes a very vivid and full color streaming high definition experience.

Tapestry of Souls - Within the Akashic Records a great monogram moving with energy and color which is a living diagram of all Souls incarnate on the planet and the Soul groups. A holographic living mural tapestry important to all life itself.

Quantum Universal Space Time Reality - This could also be explained as the Eternal Now Moment. The expanded version is a template of overlaying time lines and realities. Parallel realities and alternate realities cascading outside of our continuing reality. These versions of time contain different variations of what we're experiencing in this reality. Some similar and some very different versions. Influenced by thought energy and when not played out in this reality, sent into an alternate reality. Beyond linear time and that which linear time is part of.

Universal Expansion of Cosmic Oneness - Your personal energy within you and your energy fields have a tendency to expand and contract in reaction and response to life. As you become more expanded continually your fields will naturally start to flow and expand with more rhythmic tides of expansion and contraction. As expansion continues your energy body will adjust and arrive at a more relaxed balance between the previous levels of guarded contraction and new levels of what we call Universal Expansion.

Glossary

Akashic Records - A sanskrit term meaning sky, space or ether. A living energetic library of every past, present, future moments of every person, place or thing, animate and inanimate. Used by God and our Souls to determine the advancement, healing and karma of the lifetimes lived.

Akashic Vision - The energetic inner visionary pictures, visions and movies that are experienced during Akashic Records, readings, practices and journeys. Akashic Vision can be dream like bringing intermittent dream like images to very lucid soul frequency movies which are interactive and can stream energy into a person through the interaction with the experience.

Alternate Realities - A universe hypothesized in some cosmological models to exist along with our own universe, possibly obeying different physical laws and having the potential for the transfer of information between universes.

Ascension - The rise of the *'Christ-consciousness'* in mankind to the point that the individual is beyond the powers of reincarnation and karma. The word *'resurrection'* as found in the New Testament is best translated as 'ascension'. After millennia of reincarnation, the soul finally gets off the wheel of karma in *'ascension'*. The transformation of a person's current ego with the light body into an ascended state of existence being able to move between dimensions including the earth plane.

Asana - A body position, typically associated with the practice of Yoga, originally identified as a mastery of sitting still. In the context of Yoga practice, asana refers to two things: the place where a practitioner (or yogin, in general usage), yogi (male), or yogini (female) sits and the manner (posture) in which he/she sits. In the Yoga sutras, Patanjali suggests that asana is "to be seated in a position that is firm, but relaxed" for extended, or timeless periods.

As a repertoire of postures were promoted to exercise the body-mind over the centuries to the present day, when yoga is sought as a primarily physical exercise form, modern usage has come to include variations from lying on the back and standing on the head, to a variety of other positions. However, in the Yoga sutras, Patanjali mentions the execution of sitting with a steadfast mind for extended periods as the third of the eight limbs of Classical or Raja yoga, but does not reference standing postures or kriyās.

Yoga practitioners (even those who are adepts at various complex postures) who seek the "simple" practice of chair-less sitting generally find it impossible or surprisingly grueling to sit still for the traditional minimum of one hour (as still practiced in eastern Vipassana), some of them then dedicating their practice to sitting asana and the sensations and mind-states that arise and evaporate in extended sits.

Ascended Masters - Spiritually enlightened beings who in past incarnations were ordinary humans, but who have undergone a series of spiritual transformations. The Ascended Master Teachings refer to the Sixth Initiation as Ascension. According to the Ascended Master Teachings, a 'Master' (or 'Spiritual Master') is a human being who has taken the Fifth Initiation and is thereby capable of dwelling on the 5th dimension. An 'Ascended Master' is a human being who has taken the Sixth Initiation and is thereby capable of dwelling on the 6th dimension. An 'Ascended Master' is a human being who has regained full union with his 'I AM Presence.' When a human being has regained full union with his 'I AM Presence,' that state of full union is referred to as 'Ascension' Technically, a human being 'ascends' when he takes the Sixth Initiation.

Astral Plane - The 5th Dimension. The 'other-wordly' plane of existence closest to the 3D physical reality. This dimension acts as a go-tween for all of the many souls, spirits and entities interacting with humans or going on to experience other worlds. Also associated with psychic activity.

Awareness - having knowledge or perception of a situation or fact. Concerned and well-informed about a particular situation or development.

Ayurvedic - the traditional Hindu system of medicine, which is based on the idea of balance in bodily systems and uses diet, herbal treatment, and yogic breathing. Based around the principles of the elements: Earth, Water, Fire, Wood, Air. From Sanskrit āyus 'life' + veda 'science.'

Bhoddisatva - in Buddhism one who has attained prajna, or Enlightenment, but who postpones Nirvana in order to help others to attain Enlightenment.

Brain Waves:

Beta waves (38 - 15 Hz) - Are the brainwaves of our "normal" waking consciousness, of our outward attention, of logical, conscious and analytical thinking. High frequency beta ("splayed beta") is seen with restlessness, stress, anxiety, panic or while our inner critic or commentator is active. Splayed beta can be differentiated from the low frequency beta of the awakened mind, when thinking feels clear, alert, creative and to the point.

Alpha brainwaves (14 - 8 Hz) are seen when we are in a relaxed state, daydreaming or visualizing ("sensualising" seems to be more appropriate as imagination in all senses - hearing, kinesthetic, smell, taste etc. - stimulates alpha waves. Your visual sense may not necessarily be the strongest for you. Some people rather feel an inner knowing). We need alpha waves as the bridge to the lower frequencies of the subconscious (theta), if we want to remember the content of our dreams or our meditation, or if we want to retrieve information from our subconscious. For this reason alpha is especially important in combination with other brainwaves.

Theta brainwaves (7 - 4 Hz) Represents the subconscious. We see theta during dream sleep (REM sleep), meditation, during peak experiences and creative states. In theta we find unconscious or suppressed parts of our psyche as well as our creativity and spirituality. Theta images are usually less distinct and colorful than alpha images, sometimes of a blueish color, but they

GLOSSARY

often feel more profound and meaningful. As long as we only produce theta brainwaves, their content will stay inaccessible to our waking mind. We need alpha to bridge the gap between theta and beta brainwaves to consciously experience or remember theta content.

Delta brainwaves (3 - 0.5 Hz) Are the brainwaves of the lowest frequency and represent the unconscious. If we only produce delta we will find us in dreamless deep sleep, but we also see delta in various combinations with other brainwaves. They may then represent intuition, curiosity, a kind of radar, hunches or a "feeling" for situations and other people. Delta is often seen with people who work in therapeutic environments or professions and with people who have had traumatic experiences and have developed a "radar" for difficult situations.

Gamma brainwaves (100 - 38 Hz) were detected later than the other brainwaves, less is known about them so far. They have been seen in states of peak performance (both physical and mental), high focus and concentration and during mystic and transcendental experiences. A lot of research is currently being done on gamma brainwaves in the 40 Hz range during meditation. One of the characteristics of gamma waves is a synchronisation of activity over wide areas of the brain. Gamma brainwaves are not easy to detect because of their low amplitude and can only partly be displayed on the Mind Mirror screen. Sometimes they may be seen as a narrow frequency band at 38 Hz.

Buddhism - A religion and philosophy indigenous to the Indian subcontinent and encompasses a variety of traditions, beliefs, and practices largely based on teachings attributed to Siddhartha Gautama, who is commonly known as the Buddha (meaning *'the awakened one'* in Sanskrit and Pāli). The Buddha lived and taught in the eastern part of Indian subcontinent some time between the 6th and 4th centuries BCE. He is recognized by Buddhists as an awakened or enlightened teacher who shared his insights to help sentient beings end suffering through eliminating ignorance, craving, and hatred, by way of understanding and seeing dependent origination and no-self, and thus attain the highest happiness, nirvana. The originating teacher of Vipassana.

Bloodline - Direct line of descent; pedigree. Your ancestors, relatives and heritage.

Chakra - (in Eastern thought) each of the centers of spiritual power in the human body, seven in number along the spine from tailbone to crown of the head. From Sanskrit chakra *'wheel* or *circle'*.

Chi (also ki,ka) The vital force believed in Taoism and other Chinese doctrines, spiritual and religious practices, thought to be inherent in all things. The unimpeded circulation of chi and a balance of its negative and positive forms in the body are held to be essential to good health in traditional Chinese medicine. Literal translation: energy. Also known as ki (*Japanese*) and ka (*Egyptian*)

Clairaudience - (*French - clair meaning 'clear' and audience meaning "hearing"*) A form of clairvoyant extra-sensory perception in which a person acquires information by paranormal auditory means. The ability to hear in a paranormal manner. May refer not to actual perception of sound, but may instead indicate impressions of the "inner mental ear" or "*the 3rd ear*". Perception of sounds, voices, tones, or noises which are not normally audible. A clairaudient (person) might hear the voices or thoughts of the spirits, messages from God, angels, masters, gurus, or persons who are discarnate, or on the other side.

Clairsentience - (*French - clair meaning 'clear' and 'sentience' is*

derived from the Latin sentire, 'to feel') A form of clairvoyant extra-sensory perception wherein a person acquires psychic knowledge by feeling. One of the six special human functions mentioned in Buddhism. Refers to a person who can feel the vibration of other people. There are many different degrees of clairsentience ranging from the perception of diseases or sickness of other people *(aka medical intuitive)* to the thoughts or emotions of other people. It differs from third eye activity in that instead of vivid pictures in the mind, a very vivid feeling can form. Psychometry is related to clairsentience.*(Psyche and metric, which means 'soul-measuring')*.

Clairvoyance - (*French - clair meaning 'clear' and voyance meaning 'vision'*) is used to refer to the ability to gain information about an object, person, location or physical event through means other than the known human senses, a form of extra-sensory perception (E.S.P.). A person said to have the ability of clairvoyance is referred to as a clairvoyant -*'one who sees clearly'*.

Consciousness - The quality or state of being aware

especially within ones self. A sense of one's personal or collective identity, including the attitudes, beliefs, and sensitivities held by or considered characteristic of an individual or group. Totality of conscious states of an individual.

De ja vu - *(French - literally 'already seen')* is the impression that one has already witnessed or experienced a current situation, even though the exact circumstances of the prior encounter are unclear and were perhaps imagined. The term was coined by a French psychic researcher, Émile Boirac (1851–1917) in his book L'Avenir des sciences psychiques ('The Future of Psychic Sciences')

Deities - A being, natural, supernatural or preternatural, with superhuman powers or qualities, and who may be thought of as holy, divine, or sacred. Believers consider that they can communicate with the deity, who can respond supernaturally to their entreaties. Deities are depicted in a variety of forms, but are also frequently expressed as having human form. Deities are often thought to be immortal, and are commonly assumed to have personalities and to possess consciousness, intellects, desires, and emotions comparable but usually superior to those of humans.

Divination - (from Latin divinare *'to foresee, to be inspired by a god'*, related to divinus, divine) is the attempt to gain insight into a question or situation by way of an occultic standardized process or ritual. Used in various forms for thousands of years, diviners ascertain their interpretations of how a querent should proceed by reading signs, events, or omens, or through alleged contact with a supernatural agency. Divination can be seen as a systematic method with which to organize what appear to be disjointed, random facets of existence such that they provide insight into a problem at hand. If a distinction is to be made between divination and fortune-telling, divination has a formal or ritual and often social character, usually in a religious context, as seen in traditional African medicine; while fortune-telling is a more everyday practice for personal purposes. Particular divination methods vary by culture and religion.

DNA - *Deoxyribonucleic Acid* is a nucleic acid containing the genetic instructions used in the development and functioning of all known living organisms (with the exception of RNA viruses). The DNA segments carrying this genetic information are called genes. Likewise, other DNA sequences have structural purposes, or are involved in regulating the use of this genetic information. Along with RNA and proteins, DNA is one of the three major macromolecules that are essential for all known forms of life.

Ego - A person's sense of self-esteem or self-importance: a boost to my ego. Psychoanalysis the part of the mind that mediates between the conscious and the unconscious and is responsible for reality testing and a sense of personal identity.

Elohim - A group of special or higher order of angels who are in charge of utilizing the creation forces of the Light of Creator God. Known also to to work with the Council of Twelve and as guardians of the Akashic Records.

Empathy or Empathic ability - The action of understanding, being aware of, being sensitive to, and vicariously experiencing the feelings, thoughts, and experience of another in either the past or present time line without previously having those feelings, thoughts, and experience fully communicated in an objectively explicit manner about the person, feelings, or situation. Someone known to use empathic abilities may be referred to as an 'empath'.

Enlightenment - Spiritual revelation or deep insight into the meaning and purpose of all things, communication with or understanding of the mind of God, profound spiritual understanding or a fundamentally changed consciousness whereby everything is perceived as a unity. Freedom from desire and other worldly passions. For Hindus, as for Buddhists and Jains, enlightenment ends the cycle of reincarnation. Souls are held to enter many different bodies through the course of their existence. In each of the lives they lead they develop spiritually. Enlightenment is a state of freedom from the ignorance that causes suffering.

E.S.P. (Extra Sensory Perception) - Psychic abilities including but not limited to: mind reading, future sight, second sight, de ja vu, remote viewing, etc. Involving the acquisition or effect of past, present or future information that cannot be deduced from presently available and normally acquired sense-based information or laws of physics and/or nature.

Etherioplasma - the term is a combination of ether (the invisible energy that carries the human spirit that

Glossary

survives each death to form a new physical body) and the plasma energy that transfers the subtle electromagnetic forces from the soul to the human form that the human spirit use to help animate the human form. Etherio – plasmic. The actual measurable yet invisible energy substance of the Soul.

Familiars - Familiar spirits *(sometimes referred to simply as 'familiars')* were supernatural entities believed to assist witches and cunning folk in their practice of magic. According to folklore, they would appear in numerous guises, often as an animal, but also at times as a human or humanoid figure, and were described as *"clearly defined, three-dimensional... forms, vivid with color and animated with movement and sound"* by those alleging to have come into contact with them, unlike later descriptions of ghosts with their "smoky, undefined forms. Also referred to as Animal spirits who work with Shamans of different cultures as well as in Native American spiritualism.

Flower of Life - The Flower of Life is a name for a geometrical figure composed of multiple evenly-spaced, overlapping circles. This figure, used as a decorative motif since ancient times, forms a flower-like pattern with the symmetrical structure of a hexagon. A "Flower of Life" figure consists of seven or more overlapping circles, in which the center of each circle is on the circumference of up to six surrounding circles of the same diameter. However, the surrounding circles need not be clearly or completely drawn; in fact, some ancient symbols that are claimed as examples of the Flower of Life contain only a single circle or hexagon.

Grace - It has been defined as the divine influence which operates in humans to regenerate and sanctify, to inspire virtuous impulses, and to impart strength to endure trial and resist temptation and as an individual virtue or excellence of divine origin. It can also be perceived as divine intervention, blessings that were not asked for or even undeserved blessings.

Gregorian Time - The system of dates used by most of the world. The Gregorian calendar was proposed by the Calabrian doctor Aloysius Lilius and was decreed by, and named after, Pope Gregory XIII on 1582-02-24. It corrected the Julian calendar whose years were slightly longer than the solar year. It also replaced the lunar calendar which was also out of time with the seasons.

The correction was achieved by skipping several days as a one-off re-synchronization and then dropping three leap days every 400 hundred years. In the revised system, leap years are all years divisible by 4 but excluding those divisible by 100 but including those divisible by 400. This gives a mean calendar year of 365.2425 days = 52.1775 weeks = 8,765.82 hours = 525,949.2 minutes = 31,556,952 seconds. Leap seconds are occasionally added to this to correct for irregularities in the Earth's rotation.

Guardian Angels - An angel assigned to protect and guide a particular person or group. The appearance of guardian angels can be traced throughout all antiquity. The concept of tutelary angels and their hierarchy was extensively developed in Christianity in the 5th century by Pseudo - Dionysius the Areopagite.

Guru - a Sanskrit term for *'teacher'* or *'master'*, especially in Eastern or Indian religions. The Hindu

Glossary

guru - shishya tradition is the oral tradition or religious doctrine transmitted from teacher to student. A teacher and guide in spiritual and philosophical matters. A trusted counselor and adviser; a mentor. A personal spiritual teacher.

Hatha Yoga - Traditional hatha yoga is a holistic yogic path, including disciplines, postures (asana), purification procedures (shatkriya), gestures (mudra), breathing (pranayama), and meditation. The hatha yoga predominantly practiced in the West consists of mostly asanas understood as physical exercises. It is also recognized as a stress-reducing practice.

Hinduism - The predominant religion of the Indian subcontinent, and one of its indigenous religions. Among other practices and philosophies, Hinduism includes a wide spectrum of laws and prescriptions of *'daily morality'* based on the notion of karma, dharma, and societal norms. Hinduism is a conglomeration of distinct intellectual or philosophical points of view, rather than a rigid common set of beliefs. Hinduism is formed of diverse traditions and has no single founder. Among its direct roots is the historical Vedic religion of Iron Age India and, as such, Hinduism is often called the *'oldest living major religion'* in the world.

I Am That I Am or Holy I Am Presence - The Self begins with that which is the permanent atom of being and the cause out of which the effect proceeds. We call this cause the I AM THAT I AM, the Presence of the I AM, or the I AM Presence.

I find that God by any name can be reduced to this sense of the eternal Presence. It defines being, and I see it as a sphere of intense light that marks the point of my origin. It is the permanent part of me, of which I am very aware, and the point to which I will return at the conclusion of this life.

Incarnation - literally means embodied in flesh or taking on flesh. It refers to the conception and birth of a sentient creature (generally a human) who is the material manifestation of a soul, entity, god or God, whose original nature is non-physical. In its religious context the word is used to mean the descent from Heaven of a god, or divine being in human/animal form on Earth.

Introspection - (or internal perception) Is the self-examination of one's conscious thoughts and feelings. The process of introspection relies exclusively on the purposeful and rational self-observation of one's mental, physical, emotional and spiritual state; however, introspection is sometimes referenced in a spiritual context as the examination of one's soul. Introspection is the act of human self-reflection, and opposite to external observation.

Intuition - The ability to understand something immediately, without the need for conscious reasoning. The ability to acquire knowledge without the use of reason. The act or faculty of knowing or sensing without the use of rational processes; immediate cognition The word 'intuition' comes from the Latin word *'intueri'*, which is often roughly translated as meaning *'to look inside"* or *'to contemplate'*. Intuition may provide us with information that we cannot justify by ordinary means.

Disincarnate - Having no material body or form. Souls

Glossary

who are between lifetimes of incarnation. Unchanging, eternal, and mysterious Ein Sof (no end)

Karma - *Pali: kamma* means action, work or deed; it also refers to the principle of causality where intent and actions of an individual influence the future of that individual. Good intent and good deed contribute to good karma and future happiness, while bad intent and bad deed contribute to bad karma and future suffering. Karma is closely associated with the idea of rebirth in some schools of Asian religions. In these schools, karma in the present affects one's future in the current life, as well as the nature and quality of future lives - or, one's saṃsāra. In Hinduism & Buddhism, The total effect of a person's actions and conduct during the successive phases of the person's existence, regarded as determining the person's destiny. Once karmas are experienced and repaid, one may leave the cycle of reincarnation. Related to cause and effect and the law of attraction.

Kriya Yoga - Described by its practitioners as the ancient Yoga system revived in modern times by Mahavatar Babaji through his disciple Lahiri Mahasaya, circa 1861, and brought into popular awareness through Paramahansa Yogananda's book *'Autobiography of a Yogi'*. The system consists of a number of levels of Pranayama based on techniques that are intended to rapidly accelerate spiritual development and engender a profound state of tranquility and God-communion The term Kriya Yoga was developed in North India from an ancient tradition. The root of the Sanskrit word literally means *'to do'* and a true 'Kriya' technique always involves work with the body and the mind simultaneously. Kriya is a form of meditation involving Tantric Shakti flow of subtle energy within the practitioner's mind & body.

Kundalini - Described as a sleeping, dormant potential force in the human organism. It is one of the components of an esoteric description of the 'subtle body', which consists of nadis (energy channels), chakras (psychic centres), prana (subtle energy), and bindu (drops of essence). Kundalini is described as being coiled up at the base of the spine, usually within muladhara (base) chakra. The image given is that of a serpent coiled three and a half times around a smokey grey lingam. Each coil is said to represent one of the three gunas, with the half coil signifying transcendence. Through meditation, and various esoteric practices, such as Kundalini Yoga, Sahaja Yoga, and Kriya Yoga, the kundalini is awakened, and can rise up through the central nadi, called sushumna, that rises up inside or alongside the spine in the spinal fluid. The progress of kundalini through the different chakras leads to different levels of awakening and mystical experience, until the kundalini finally reaches the top of the head, Sahasrara chakra, producing an extremely profound mystical experience that is said to be indescribable.

Knowing Way of Truth and Light - The original Christ teachings which came from Atlantis. Also known as the Way Teachings, The Way, The Knowing Way.

Love - An emotion of a strong affection and personal attachment. Love is also a virtue representing all of human kindness, compassion, and affection - The

GLOSSARY

unselfish loyal and benevolent concern for the good of another. Love may describe actions towards others or oneself based on compassion or affection. Love refers to a variety of different feelings, states, and attitudes, ranging from pleasure (*"I loved that meal"*) to interpersonal attraction (*"I love my partner"*). 'Love' may refer specifically to the passionate desire and intimacy of romantic love, to the sexual love of eros, to the emotional closeness of family love, to the platonic love that defines friendship, or to the profound oneness or devotion of religious love, or to a concept of love that encompasses all of those feelings. This diversity of uses and meanings, combined with the complexity of the feelings involved, makes love unusually difficult to consistently define, compared to other emotional states. Love in its various forms acts as a major facilitator of interpersonal relationships and, owing to its central psychological importance, is one of the most common themes in the creative arts.

Lymph (glands) - Physiology a colorless fluid containing white blood cells, that bathes the tissues and drains through the lymphatic system into the bloodstream. Fluid exuding from a sore or inflamed tissue. Literary pure water.

Mala - A string of beads worn around the neck or wrist, traditionally of 108 bead count, to be used for prayers, mantras and chants. From the ancient Eastern traditions, and can also refer to a catholic rosary.

Mandala - A Sanskrit word meaning *'circle.'* In the Buddhist and Hindu religious traditions sacred art often takes a mandala form. The basic form of most Hindu and Buddhist mandalas is a square with four gates containing a circle with a center point. Each gate is in the shape of a T. Mandalas often exhibit radial balance. These mandalas, concentric diagrams, have spiritual and ritual significance in both Buddhism and Hinduism.

The term is of Hindu origin and appears in the Rig Veda as the name of the sections of the work, but is also used in other Indian religions, particularly Buddhism. In the Tibetan branch of Vajrayana Buddhism, mandalas have been developed into sand painting. They are also a key part of anuttara yoga tantra meditation practices. In various spiritual traditions, mandalas may be employed for focusing attention of aspirants and adepts, as a spiritual teaching tool, for establishing a sacred space, and as an aid to meditation and trance induction. It's symbolic nature can help one "to access progressively deeper levels of the unconscious, ultimately assisting the meditator to experience a mystical sense of oneness with the ultimate unity from which the cosmos in all its manifold forms arises." The psychoanalyst Carl Jung saw the mandala as *"a representation of the unconscious self,"* and believed his paintings of mandalas enabled him to identify emotional disorders and work towards wholeness in personality.

Mantras - a sound, seed sound, syllable, word, or group of words that is considered capable of creating (spiritual) transformation when used as a written or chanted prayer. A sacred verbal formula repeated in prayer, meditation, or incantation, such as an invocation of God, a magic spell, or a syllable or portion of scripture containing mystical potentialities. Chanted

Glossary

individually and in groups both silently and aloud traditionally 108 times and with the use of a mala or prayer beads.

Mediumship - Involves a cooperating effort between a person on the Earth plane (the medium or channel) and a person in Spirit (the communicator).

Mudras - In Sanskrit: *'seal'*, *'mark'*, or *'gesture'*; Tibetan, *chakgya* is a symbolic or ritual gesture in Hinduism and Buddhism. While some mudrās involve the entire body, most are performed with the hands and fingers. A mudrā is a spiritual gesture and an energetic seal of authenticity employed in the iconography and spiritual practice of Indian religions and traditions of Dharma and Taoism. One hundred and eight mudrasare used in regular Tantric rituals. In yoga, mudrās are used in conjunction with pranayama (yogic breathing exercises), generally while seated in Padmasana, Sukhasana or Vajrasana pose, to stimulate different parts of the body involved with breathing and to affect the flow of prana in the body.

Meditation - A practice in which an individual trains the mind or induces a mode of consciousness, either to realize some benefit or as an end in itself. The term meditation refers to a broad variety of practices (much like the term sports) that includes techniques designed to promote relaxation, build internal energy or life force (qi, ki, prana, etc.) and develop compassion, love, patience, generosity and forgiveness. A particularly ambitious form of meditation aims at effortlessly sustained single-pointed concentration single-pointed analysis, meant to enable its practitioner to enjoy an indestructible sense of well-being while engaging in any life activity.

Metatron's Cube - The name of Metatron's Cube makes reference to Metatron, an angel mentioned in apocryphal texts including the Second Book of Enoch and the Book of the Palaces. These texts rank Metatron second only to the Abrahamic God in the hierarchy of spiritual beings. The derivation of Metatron's cube from the tree of life, which the Talmud clearly states was excluded from human experience during the exile from Eden.

Metatron's cube contains every shape that exists in the universe God has created, and those shapes are the building blocks of all physical matter, which are known as Platonic solids (because the philosopher Plato linked them to the spirit world of heaven and the physical elements on Earth).

The pattern delineated by many of the lines can be created by orthographic projections of the first three Platonic solids. Specifically, the line pattern includes projections of a double tetrahedron (aka stellated octahedron), a cube within a cube (a three-dimensional projection of a tesseract), and an octahedron.

Monad - Was a term for Divinity or the first being, or the totality of all beings. Monad being the source or the One meaning without division.

Mysticism - from the Greek, mystikos, meaning 'an initiate') is the knowledge of, and especially the personal experience of, states of consciousness, or levels of being, or aspects of reality, beyond normal human perception, including experience of and even communion with a

Glossary

supreme being.

Neocortex - The neocortex consists of the grey matter, or neuronal cell bodies and unmyelinated fibers, surrounding the deeper white matter (myelinated axons) in the cerebrum. The neocortex is smooth in rodents and other small mammals, whereas in primates and other larger mammals it has deep grooves (sulci) and wrinkles (gyri). These folds allow the surface area of the neocortex to increase far beyond what could otherwise be fit in the same size skull. All human brains have the same overall pattern of main gyri and sulci, although they differ in detail from one person to another. The mechanism by which the gyri form during embryogenesis is not entirely clear. However, it may be due to differences in cellular proliferation rates in different areas of the cortex early in embryonic development.

Om or Aum - is a mystical sound of Sanskrit origin, sacred and important in various Dharmic religions such as Hinduism, Buddhism, and Jainism. It is placed at the beginning of most Hindu texts as a sacred incantation to be intoned at the beginning and end of a reading of the Vedas or prior to any prayer or mantra. It is used at the end of the invocation to the god being sacrificed to (anuvakya) as an invitation to and for that God to partake of the sacrifice. The Māndukya Upanishad is entirely devoted to the explanation of the syllable. The syllable consists of three phonemes, a (Vaishvanara), u (Hiranyagarbha), and m(Ishvara), which symbolize the beginning, duration, and dissolution of the universe and the associated gods Brahma, Vishnu, and Shiva, respectively. The name omkara is taken as a name of

God in the Hindu revivalist Arya Samaj and can be translated as *"I Am Existence"*. Also referred to as the primordial vibrational tone behind all realities and dimensions. Monks and Siddhas have reported to hear this tone vibrating in the deepest levels of trance and meditation.

Om Mani Padme Hum - *"The jewel of consciousness is in the lotus of my heart"* and *"I bow to the light within"* are meditative translations to focus upon while using this mantra. Om coincides with the 3rd eye and forehead, Mani - back of the head, Padme - heart and Hum - throat. Visualizing a ring of God's Divine light through these centers while chanting this mantra clears away negativity, pain, fear and stress and brings compassion and healing to the heart, mind and body, while opening and blending what the higher teachings refer to as the Heart/Mind. Tibetan Buddhists believe that saying this mantra (prayer), Om Mani Padme Hum, out loud or silently to oneself, invokes the powerful benevolent attention and blessings of Chenrezig, the embodiment of compassion. Viewing the written form of the mantra is said to have the same effect. It is said that all the teachings of the Buddha are contained in this mantra.

According to the Dali Lama: "It is very good to recite the mantra **Om Mani Padme Hum**, but while you are doing it, you should be thinking on it's meaning, for the meaning of the six syllables is great and vast... The first, *'Om'* symbolizes the practitioner's impure body, speech, and mind; it also symbolizes the pure exalted body, speech, and mind of a Buddha. The path is indicated by the next four syllables. *'Mani'*, meaning jewel, symbolizes the factors of method: (the) altruistic intention to become enlightened, compassion, and love. The two syllables, *'Padme'*, meaning lotus, symbolize wisdom. Purity must be achieved by an indivisible unity of method and wisdom, symbolized by the final syllable *'Hum'*, which indicates indivisibility. Thus the six syllables, *'Om Mani Padme Hum'*, mean that in dependence on the practice of a path which is an indivisible union of method and wisdom, you can transform your impure body, speech, and mind into the pure exalted body, speech, and mind of a Buddha"

Omnipresence - The property of being present everywhere. This characteristic is most commonly used in a religious context, as most doctrines bestow the trait of omnipresence onto a superior, a deity or God. This also identifies the universe and divinity; in divine omnipresence, the divine and universe are separate, but the divine is present everywhere.

Hinduism, and other religions that derive from it, incorporate the theory of transcendent and immanent omnipresence which is the traditional meaning of the word, Brahman. This theory defines a universal and fundamental substance, which is the source of all physical existence. Divine omnipresence is thus one of the divine attributes.

Past Lives - According to the study of reincarnation, the lives that our soul has previously lived or participated in. Past lives can be incarnations within the same family or within different races and regions of the world. These past lives are often discoverable through dreams, past life regression, Shamanic Journeys and Journeys into the Akashic Records and a person's Book of Lifetimes.

Pan Fairy Realm - The 2nd Dimensional beings that often interact with nature. Fairies, gnomes, earth and nature devas that assist mother earth in tending her planetary garden. Intermittently these being can find their way into human incarnation by way of evolution. Often these folks can feel a deep bond with mother nature without knowing why. Some incarnate knowing where they came from.

Pineal Gland - (or the *'third eye'*) is a small endocrine gland in the brain. It produces the serotonin derivative melatonin, a hormone that affects the modulation of wake/sleep patterns and seasonal functions. Its shape resembles a tiny pine cone (hence its name), and it is located near the centre of the brain, between the two hemispheres, tucked in a groove where the two rounded thalamic bodies join. The Pineal Gland has for long been associated with Esoteric Knowledge surrounding the spiritual, metaphysical aspects of consciousness and the self. René Descartes, who dedicated much time to the study of the pineal gland, called it the *'Seat of the Soul'*. He believed that it was the point of connection between the intellect and the body.

Directly behind the root of the nose (3rd eye chakra) floating in a small lake of cerebrospinal fluid. It is our body's biological clock. The pineal gland has been supplied with the best blood, oxygen and nutrient mix available other than that received by our kidneys. It acts as a receiving mechanism capable of monitoring electromagnetic fields and helping align bodies in space. With its central hormone, Melatonin, the pineal not only

GLOSSARY

regulates sleep/wake cycles and the aging process, but also appears to act as the Mistress Gland (sofia)* orchestrating the body's entire endocrine system and thus, energetically speaking, the chakra system. It is also responsible for shamanic states, visions, kundalini awakening e.t.c.

Pituitary Gland - An endocrine gland about the size of a pea and weighing 0.5 grams (0.018 oz) in humans. It is not a part of the brain. It is a protrusion off the bottom of the hypothalamus at the base of the brain, and rests in a small, bony cavity (sella turcica) covered by a dural fold (diaphragma sellae). The pituitary is functionally connected to the hypothalamus by the median eminence via a small tube called the infundibular stem (Pituitary stalk). The pituitary fossa, in which the pituitary gland sits, is situated in the sphenoid bone in the middle cranial fossa at the base of the brain.

The pituitary gland secretes nine hormones that regulate homeostasis. The Pituitary Gland is known as the Master Gland of the Endocrine System. It's secretions regulate all the other Endocrine Glands. This gland represents one's ability to coordinate the different aspects of one's Life. Problems represent difficulty doing this. The Pituitary Gland is linked to the Hypothalamus, also located in the brain, whose function is to maintain Homeostasis in the body. That is the body's tendency to return automatically to its level of highest functioning. Metaphysically, this means aligning the frequencies of the physical and energetic bodies to homeostatically return to one's highest spiritual functioning. The pituitary gland is called the *"Seat of the Mind"* with the frontal lobe regulating emotional thoughts such as poetry and music, and the anterior lobe regulating concrete thought and intellectual concepts. The pineal gland is known as the *'Seat of Illumination, Intuition and Cosmic Consciousness'*. The pineal gland is to the pituitary gland what intuition is to reason. The glandular system also coincides with the chakra system.

Prana - The Sanskrit word for *'vital life'* (from the root prā 'to fill',). It is one of the five organs of vitality or sensation, prana *"breath"*, vac *'speech'*, chakshus *'sight'*, shrotra *'hearing'*, and manas *'thought'* (nose, mouth, eyes, ears and mind). In Vedantic philosophy, prana is the notion of a vital, life-sustaining force of living beings and vital energy, comparable to the Chinese notion of Qi. Prana is a central concept in Hinduism, particularly in Ayurveda and Yoga. It flows through a network of fine subtle channels called nadis. Its most subtle material form is the breath, but it is also to be found in the blood, and its most concentrated form is semen in men and vaginal fluid in women. Prana was first expounded in the Upanishads, where it is part of the worldly, physical realm, sustaining the body and the mother of thought and thus also of the mind. Prana suffuses all living forms but is not itself the Atman or individual soul. In the Ayurveda, the Sun and sunshine are held to be a source of prana.

Pranayama - A Sanskrit word meaning 'extension of the prana or breath' or more accurately, *'extension of the life force'*. The word is composed of two Sanskrit words,

Prāna, life force, or vital energy, particularly, the breath, and 'ayāma', to extend or draw out.

Psyche - The totality of the human mind, conscious, and unconscious. Psychology is the scientific or objective study of the psyche. The word has a long history of use in psychology and philosophy, dating back to ancient times, and has been one of the fundamental concepts for understanding human nature from a scientific point of view.

Psychic - Relating to or denoting faculties or phenomena that are apparently inexplicable by natural laws, especially involving telepathy or clairvoyance: psychic powers. A person appearing or considered to have powers of telepathy or clairvoyance. Of or relating to the soul or mind. From the Greek psychikos—'*of the mind, mental*', is a person who possesses an ability to perceive information hidden from the normal senses through extrasensory perception (ESP), It can also denote an ability of the mind to influence the world physically using psychokinetic powers.

Elaborate systems of divination and fortune - telling date back to ancient times. Perhaps the most widely-known system of early civilization fortune - telling was astrology, where practitioners believed the relative positions of celestial bodies could lend insight into people's lives and even predict their future circumstances. Some fortune-tellers were said to be able to make predictions without the use of ritualistic objects or special, spiritual, or energy tools for diving information. More so through direct apprehension or vision of the past, present or future. These people were known as seers or prophets, and in later times as clairvoyants and psychics.

Qi Gong - a practice of aligning breath, movement, and awareness for exercise, healing, and meditation. With roots in Chinese medicine, martial arts, and philosophy, qigong is traditionally viewed as a practice to cultivate and balance qi (chi) or what has been translated as *'intrinsic life energy'*. Typically a Qigong practice involves rhythmic breathing coordinated with slow stylized repetition of fluid movement, a calm mindful state, and visualization of guiding qi through the body. Qigong is now practiced throughout China and worldwide, and is considered by some to be exercise, and by others to be a type of alternative medicine or meditative practice. From a philosophical perspective Qigong is believed to help develop human potential, allow access to higher realms of awareness, and awaken one's 'true nature'.

Quantum Physics - The study of the behaviour of matter and energy at the molecular, atomic, nuclear, and even smaller microscopic levels. In the early 20th century, it was discovered that the laws that govern macroscopic objects do not function the same in such small realms. In the realm of quantum physics, observing something actually influences the physical processes taking place. Light waves act like particles and particles act like waves (called wave particle duality). Matter can go from one spot to another without moving through the intervening space (called quantum tunnelling). Information moves instantly across vast distances. In fact, in quantum mechanics we discover that the entire

Glossary

universe is actually a series of probabilities.

R.E.M. (raphid eye movement) - REM sleep typically occupies 20–25% of total sleep, about 90–120 minutes of a night's sleep. REM sleep is considered the deepest stage of sleep, and normally occurs close to morning. During a night of sleep, one usually experiences about four or five periods of REM sleep; they are quite short at the beginning of the night and longer toward the end. Many animals and some people tend to wake, or experience a period of very light sleep, for a short time immediately after a bout of REM. The relative amount of REM sleep varies considerably with age. A newborn baby spends more than 80% of total sleep time in REM. During REM, the activity of the brain's neurons is quite similar to that during waking hours; for this reason, the REM-sleep stage may be called paradoxical sleep.

Rosicrucians - Studies or membership within a philosophical secret society said to have been founded in late medieval Germany by Christian Rosenkreuz. It holds a doctrine or theology "built on esoteric truths of the ancient past", which, "concealed from the average man, provide insight into nature, the physical universe and the spiritual realm." Rosicrucianism is symbolized by the Rosy Cross. In the early 17th century, the manifestos caused excitement throughout Europe by declaring the existence of a secret brotherhood of alchemists and sages who were preparing to transform the arts, sciences, religion, and political and intellectual landscape of Europe. Wars of politics and religion ravaged the continent. The works were re-issued several times and followed by numerous pamphlets, favorable and otherwise. Between 1614 and 1620, about 400 manuscripts and books were published which discussed the Rosicrucian documents.

Samadhi - Described as a non-dualistic state of consciousness in which the consciousness of the experiencing subject becomes one with the experienced object, and in which the mind becomes still, one-pointed or concentrated while the person remains conscious. In Buddhism, it can also refer to an abiding in which mind becomes very still but does not merge with the object of attention, and is thus able to observe and gain insight into the changing flow of experience. In Hinduism, samādhi can also refer to videha mukti or the complete absorption of the individual consciousness in the self at the time of death, usually referred to as mahasamādhi.

Sanskrit - Classical Sanskrit is the standard register as laid out in the grammar of Pāṇini, 4th century BCE and it has significantly influenced most modern languages of the Indian subcontinent, particularly in India, Pakistan, Sri Lanka and Nepal. The pre-Classical form of Sanskrit is known as Vedic Sanskrit, with the language of the Rigveda being the oldest and most archaic stage preserved, its oldest core dating back to as early as 1500 BCE. This qualifies Rigvedic Sanskrit as one of the oldest attestations of any Indo-Iranian language, and one of the earliest attested members of the Indo-European language family.

Siddha - A Siddham in Tamil(an Indian sub-continent dialect) means *'one who is accomplished'* and refers to perfected masters who, according to Hindu belief, have transcended the ahamkara (ego or I-maker), have subdued their minds to be subservient to their Awareness, and have transformed their bodies (composed mainly of dense Rajo-tama gunas) into a different kind of body dominated by sattva. This is usually accomplished only by persistent meditation. Siddhas are the liberated souls. They have completely ended the cycle of birth and death. They have reached the ultimate state of salvation. They do not have any karmas and they do not collect any new karmas. This state of true freedom is called Moksha. They are formless and have no passions and therefore are free from all temptations. A siddha has also been defined to refer to one who has attained a siddhi.

Siddhi - The siddhis as paranormal abilities are considered emergent abilities of an individual that is on the path to siddhahood, and do not define a siddha, who is established in the Pranav or Aum – the spiritual substrate of creation. The siddhi in its pure form means "the attainment of flawless identity with Reality (Brahman); perfection of Spirit." In the Hindu philosophy of Kashmir Shaivism (Hindu tantra), siddha also refers to a Siddha Guru who can by way of Shaktipat initiate disciples into Yoga.

Soul or **Soul Group** - The incorporeal and immortal essence of a person, living thing, or object. Souls which are immortal and capable of union with the divine belong only to human beings. 12 Souls are grouped together in a Soul Group which is governed by an Over Soul. 12 Soul Groups are governed by a Monad.

Solar Gazing - Hira Ratan Manek (HRM), among

others, have proven eating any food. The method is used for curing all kinds of psychosomatic, mental and physical illnesses as well as increasing memory power and mental strength by using sunlight. One can get rid of any kind of psychological problems, and develop confidence to face any problem in life and can overcome any kind of fear including that of death within 3 months after starting to practice this method. As a result, one will be free from mental disturbances and fear, which will result in a perfect balance of mind.

If one continues to apply the proper sun gazing practice for 6 months, they will be free from physical illnesses. Furthermore, after 9 months, one can eventually win a victory over hunger, which disappears by itself thereafter. This is a straight-forward yet effective method based on solar energy, which enables one to harmonize and recharge the body with life energy and also invoke the unlimited powers of the mind very easily. Additionally, it allows one to easily liberate from threefold sufferings of humanity such as mental illnesses, physical illnesses and spiritual ignorance.

Spirit Guides - A term used by the Western tradition of Spiritualist Churches, mediums, and psychics to describe an entity that remains a dis-incarnate spirit in order to act as a guide or protector to a living incarnated human being. Traditionally, within the spiritualist churches, spirit guides were often stereotyped ethnically, with Native Americans, Chinese or Egyptians being popular for their perceived ancient wisdom. Other popular types of guides were saints or other enlightened individuals. The term can also refer to totems, angels, guardian angels or nature spirits.

    Spirit guides are not always of human descent. Some spirit guides live as energy, in the cosmic realm, or as light beings, which are very high level spirit guides. Some spirit guides are persons who have lived many former lifetimes, paid their karmic debts, and advanced beyond a need to reincarnate. Many devotees believe that spirit guides are chosen on "the other side" by human beings who are about to incarnate and wish assistance.

    Tai Chi - A type of internal Chinese martial art practiced for both its defense training and its health benefits. It is also typically practiced for a variety of other personal reasons: its hard and soft martial art technique, demonstration competitions, and longevity. As a result, a multitude of training forms exist, both traditional and modern, which correspond to those aims. Some of Tai Chi Chuan's training forms are especially known for being practiced at what most people categorize as slow movement.

    Tantra or **tantric** - Defined primarily as a technique-rich style of spiritual practice, Tantra has no single coherent doctrine; rather, it developed different teachings in connection with the different religions that adopted the Tantric method. These teachings tended to support and validate the practices of Tantra, which in their classical form are more oriented to the married householder than the monastic or solitary renunciant, and thus exhibited what may be called a world-embracing rather than a world-denying character. Thus Tantra, especially in its nondual forms, rejected the renunciant values of Patañjalian yoga, offering instead a vision of the whole of reality as the self-expression of a single, free and blissful Divine Consciousness under whatever name, whether Śiva or Buddha-nature.

Since the world was viewed as real, not illusory, this doctrine was a significant innovation over and against previous Indian philosophies, which tended to picture the Divine as absolutely transcendent and/or the world as illusion. The practical consequence of this view was that not only could householders aspire to spiritual liberation in the Tantric system, they were the type of practitioner that most Tantric manuals had in mind. Furthermore, since Tantra dissolved the dichotomy of spiritual versus mundane, practitioners could entail every aspect of their daily lives into their spiritual growth process, seeking to realize the transcendent in the immanent.

Tantric spiritual practices and rituals thus aim to bring about an inner realization of the truth that *"Nothing exists that is not Divine"* (nāśivaṃ vidyate kvacit), bringing freedom from ignorance and from the cycle of suffering (saṃsāra) in the process. In fact, tantric visualizations are said to bring the meditator to the core of his humanity and oneness with transcendence. Tantric meditations do not serve the function of training or practicing extra beliefs or unnatural ways. On the contrary, the transcendence that is reached by such meditative work does not construct anything in the mind of the practitioner, but actually de-constructs all preconceived notions of the human condition. The barriers that constrict thinking to limitation, namely, cultural and linguistic frameworks are completely removed. This allows the person to experience total liberation and then unity with ultimate truth or reality.

Thymus gland - The thymus is a specialized organ of the immune system. The thymus *"educates"* T-lymphocytes (T cells), which are critical cells of the adaptive immune system. Each T cell attacks a foreign substance which it identifies with its receptor. T cells have receptors which are generated by randomly shuffling gene segments. Each T cell attacks a different antigen. T cells that attack the body's own proteins are eliminated in the thymus. Thymic epithelial cells express major proteins from elsewhere in the body, and T cells that respond to those proteins are eliminated through programmed cell death (apoptosis). The thymus is composed of two identical lobes and is located in front of the heart and behind the sternum.

Tao - A Chinese word meaning *'way'*, *'path'*, *'route'*, or sometimes more loosely, *'doctrine'* or *'principle'*. Within the context of traditional Chinese philosophy and religion, Tao is a metaphysical concept originating with Laozi that gave rise to a religion (Wade–Giles, Tao Chiao; Pinyin, Daojiao) and philosophy (Wade–Giles, Tao chia; Pinyin, Daojia) referred to in English with the single term Taoism. The concept of Tao was later adopted in Confucianism, Chán and Zen Buddhism and more broadly throughout East Asian philosophy and religion in general. Within these contexts Tao signifies the primordial essence or fundamental nature of the universe. In the foundational text of Taoism, the Tao Te Ching, Laozi explains that Tao is not a *'name'* for a *'thing'* but the underlying natural order of the universe whose ultimate essence is difficult to circumscribe. Tao is thus *'eternally nameless'* (Dao De Jing-32. Laozi) and to be distinguished from the countless 'named' things which are considered to be its manifestations.

Violet Flame - The Violet Flame is a Divine gift and tool for everyone, given to us by Ascended Master Saint Germain. It is a sacred fire that exists on the Higher Dimensions. People with the gift of inter-dimensional sight have seen it. Cameras have captured it when it was not visible to the person taking the photo. The Violet Flame is REAL and I invite you to use it to your great advantage. The Violet Flame is Spiritual Alchemy in action. Just as Alchemy is said to turn Lead into Gold, the ultimate purpose of the Violet Flame is to turn the Human into the Divine Human. Its action is to TRANSMUTE denser feelings, actions, deeds, karma, etc. into a higher vibrational frequency, which helps prepare us for our Ascension

Vipassana - In the Buddhist tradition means insight into the true nature of reality. A regular practitioner of Vipassana, is known as a Vipassi. Vipassana is one of the world's most ancient techniques of meditation, which was introduced by Gautama Buddha. It is a practice of self-transformation through self-observation and introspection to the extent that sitting with a steadfast mind becomes an active experience of change and impermanence. In the west, Vipassanā meditation is often referred to simply as *"insight meditation"*.

Wheel of Life - The bhavacakra (Sanskrit; Pali: bhavacakka; Tibetan: srid pa'i 'khor lo) is a symbolic

GLOSSARY

representation of samsara (or cyclic existence) found on the outside walls of Tibetan Buddhist temples and monasteries in the Indo-Tibetan region. In the Mahayana Buddhist tradition, it is believed that the drawing was designed by the Buddha himself in order to help ordinary people understand the Buddhist teachings. The bhavacakra is popularly referred to as the wheel of life. This term is also translated as wheel of cyclic existence or wheel of becoming.

Yantra - Is the Sanskrit word for "instrument" or "machine". Much like the word "instrument" itself, it can stand for symbols, processes, automata, machinery or anything that has structure and organization, depending on context. One usage popular in the west is as symbols or geometric figures. Traditionally such symbols are used in Eastern mysticism to balance the mind or focus it on spiritual concepts. The act of wearing, depicting, enacting and/or concentrating on a yantra is held to have spiritual, astrological or magical benefits in the Tantric traditions of the Indian religions.

PRODUCTS & SERVICES

Experience the Special Edition Journey to the Akashic Records

- 390 pages 2 Glossaries
- Multiple meditation and energy techniques
- Multiple Akashic Guided Journeys
- Never Before Shared Information concerning the streaming of the Akashic Records and your Soul's connection to it!
- Many new Perspectives.

Available at billfoss.net and Amazon

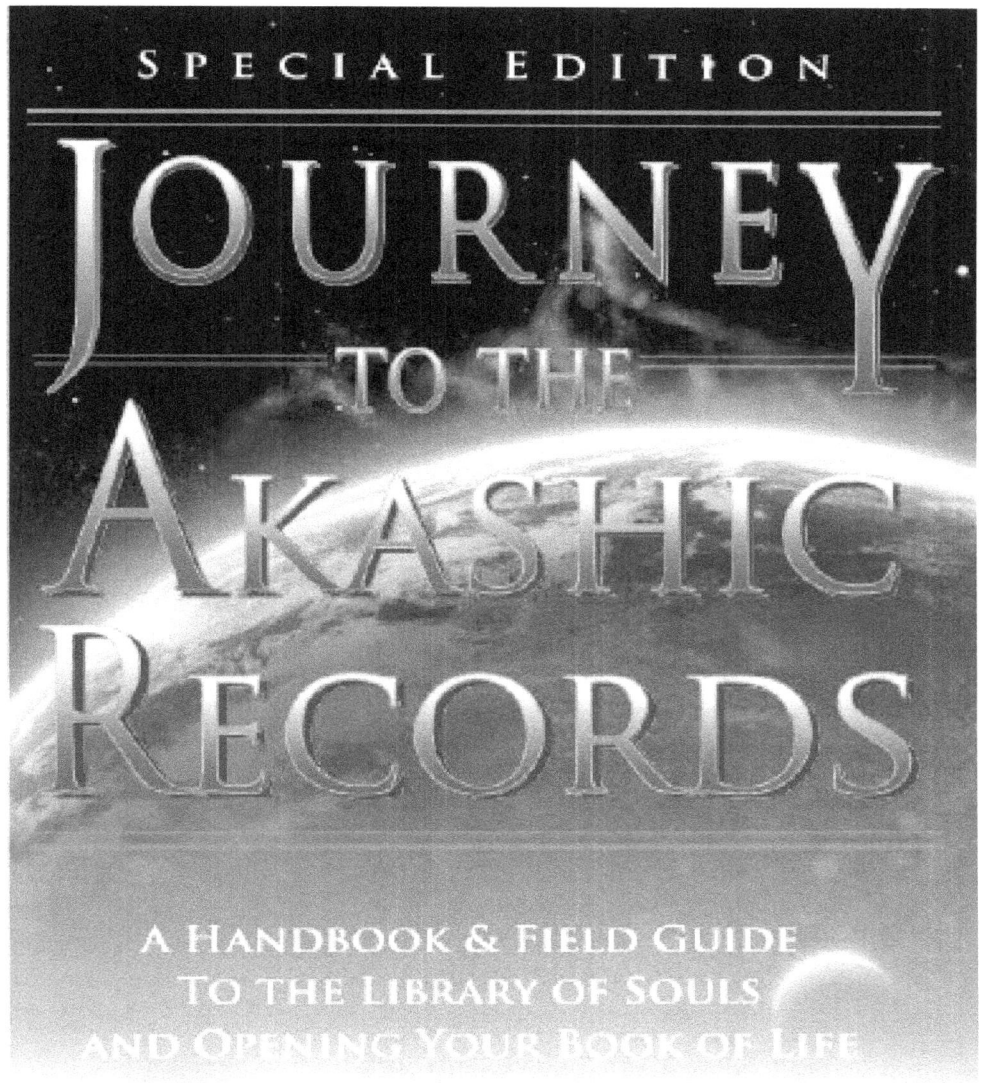

Products & Services

Check out the monthly newsletter for:
- Meditation insights and tips
- Upcoming workshop locations
- Personal individual sessions
- CD's and Downloads
- New Art & More!

www.billfoss.net

Products & Services

The "Journey to the Akashic Records" Study Set!
For Home Study and the Workshops Into the Akashic Records!
Available at billfoss.net

Akashic Records, Healing, and Personal Guidance Phone Sessions

Bill works with you in person when available or by phone to unlock your greatest potential, give life path guidance, for personal healing and manifesting your goals and dreams in life. Looking into your personal Book of Life within the Akashic Records. This enables you to see tendencies from other lifetimes as they are played out in the multi-dimensional reality that makes up who you are. Channeled information from the Records, with the aid of your spirit guides, angelics, and ascended masters or spiritual gurus, reveal information that make up who you are on the otherside, as well as in the physical. This can bring clarity to your current situation. As you state your questions, Your answers will come from the Akashic Records and will give clarity to the reasons for the immediate events and circumstances as well as how to navigate more clearly and receive info for business and personal relations, spiritual attainment, and locations, Past, Present and Future.

Book your Session: **www.billfoss.net**

"If you need help in getting to the next level on your journey, This will be beneficial for you."

PRODUCTS & SERVICES

The "Journey to the Akasha" Guided Journey Set
Study, Practice, and Learn New Ways of Opening
Into the Akashic Records - 4 CD's
Available from www.billfoss.net or Amazon

PRODUCTS & SERVICES

The "Journey to the Akasha" Workbook!
Study, Practice, and Learn New Ways of Opening Into the Akashic Records!
Available at billfoss.net or Amazon

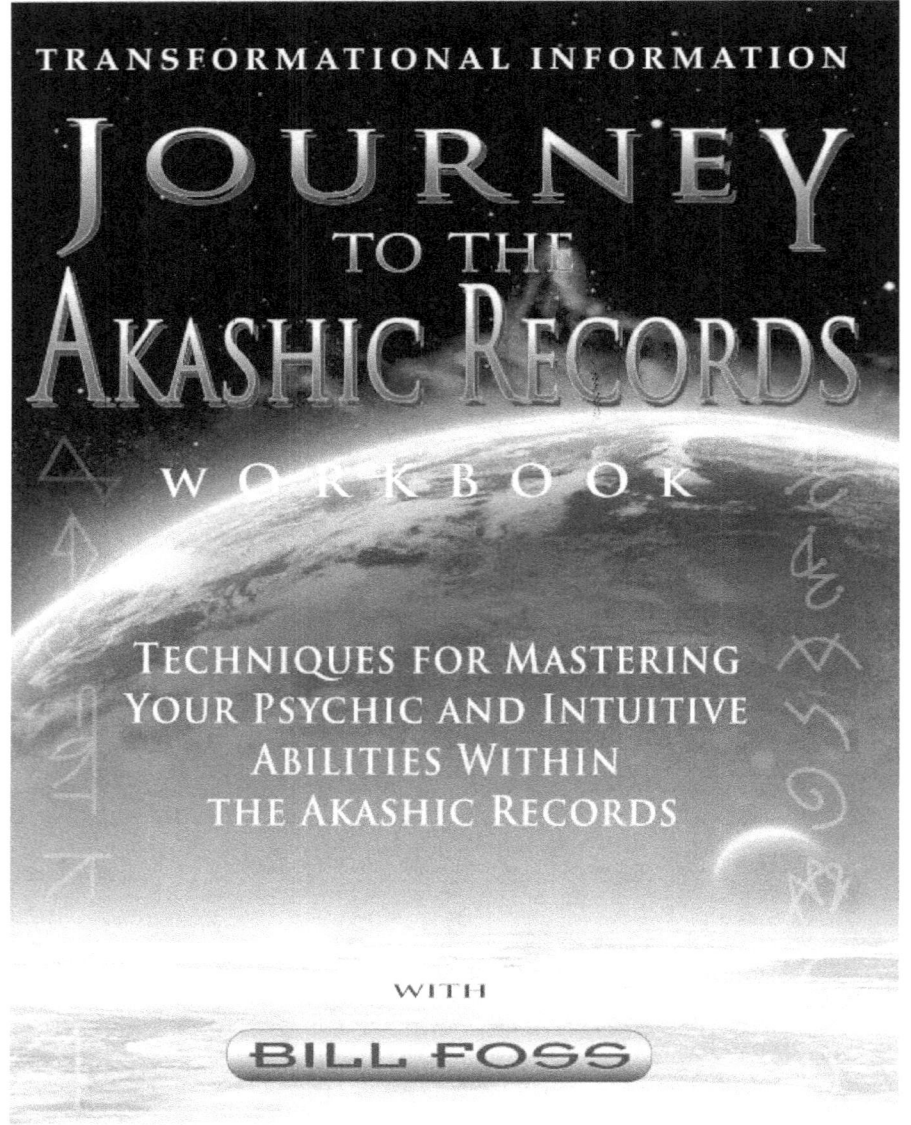

The "Journey to the Akasha" Workbook, Is the study companion workbook for all the exercises at the workshops, presentations and classes. This workbook will help you open and expand your abilities while giving you insight to strengthen your practice or working with your intuitive and healing abilities. Size 8.5" x 11" 165 Pages

PRODUCTS & SERVICES

Meditation & Music CDs & Downloads

billfoss.net

Products & Services

The Secrets of Spiritual Success is a clear and concise road map providing an overview of understanding of 1000's of years of spiritual teachings, inquiries, and understandings. This book will help you to connect the dots more quickly in life, while adding to your studies already in motion or providing a great primer source to get started from. Whether you are a mystical student from beyond or you are new to expanded views and just looking for answers, this book was created to enliven and enrich your search, practices and studies. This book will turn on the lights for you and keep them on." Size 6" x 9" 237 Pages

PRODUCTS & SERVICES

Book • Workbook • Journal
Complete Study Set - Order at www.billfoss.net

"The Keys of Spiritual Success" Workbook, companion to "The Secrets of Spiritual Success" is a collection of creative visualization and healing techniques, energy exercises, meditations, prayers. Exercises and insights to jump start your journey into your own long awaited or continued self inquiry and realization. Use this Workbook to Journal your subtle and not so subtle experiences as you open to greater understandings, fresh ideas, and new ways of being!" Size 8.5" x 11" 165 Pages

"The "Book Of Dreams" Journal is your gateway into creativity. This is your Journal, your space to create. What will you write, sketch, plan, or invent? Take the opportunity to go within and explore the vast regions, depths, and banks of Divine Creative Potential existing within you, all around you, throughout time, space & beyond. This is your chance to write down, plan and draw out your dream and make it a reality. Use this book as you will to expand your vision. It all starts here, and it starts with you so let's begin. Size 8.5" x 11" 165 Pages

Art Prints of the Spiritual Masters
*Originals and Special Orders Available
at www.billfossworld.com*

Notes:

Notes:

Notes:

www.ingramcontent.com/pod-product-compliance
Lightning Source LLC
Chambersburg PA
CBHW080545230426
43663CB00015B/2712